The Internet Start-Up Bible

Tess Read, Calum Chace and Simon Rowe

RANDOM HOUSE
BUSINESS BOOKS

First published in 2000 by Random House Business Books,
Random House, 20 Vauxhall Bridge Road, London SW1V 2SA

Random House Australia (Pty) Limited
20 Alfred Street, Milsons Point,
Sydney, New South Wales 2061, Australia

Random House New Zealand Limited
18 Poland Road, Glenfield,
Auckland 10, New Zealand

Random House (Pty) Limited
Endulini, 5a Jubilee Road, Parktown 2193, South Africa

The Random House Group Limited Reg. No. 954009

Papers used by Random House are natural, recyclable products
made from wood grown in sustainable forests. The manufacturing processes
conform to the environmental regulations of the country of origin.

ISBN 0 7126 6966 3

Companies, institutions and other organizations wishing to make
bulk purchases of books published by Random House should
contact their local bookstore or Random House direct:
Special Sales Director
Random House, 20 Vauxhall Bridge Road, London SW1V 2SA
Tel 020 7840 8470   Fax 020 7828 6681

www.randomhouse.co.uk
businessbooks@randomhouse.co.uk

Typeset in Garamond Light & News Gothic by
MATS, Southend-on-Sea, Essex
Printed and bound in Great Britain by
Biddles Ltd, Guildford and King's Lynn

Contents

Foreword

The 'dot' in .com is there for a very good reason. Metaphorically, it is a reminder to pause before leaping into the exciting but risky world of e-commerce. Rush headlong, driven by enthusiasm and on the engine of hype, at your peril. Stop, pause, and plan. You will have a far better chance of succeeding. Consider this book the dot in your .com.

The internet, by design, is a great leveller. At Viant, we have spent the last four years helping some of the world's largest companies (General Motors, American Express, Diageo) and some of its smallest companies (della.com, sputnik7.com, planetLingo.com) leverage the potential of the new digital economy. We know that it is access to this level playing field that offers everyone the opportunity of success. But we also know that this unfettered access presents a great challenge. At the moment, anyone with a '.com' or a '.co.uk' in their business plan seems to have unlimited access to capital, but they also have an 'all areas access' pass to a chasm littered with the detritus of great, but poorly executed, ideas.

The bridge across this chasm is a detailed, realistic and actionable business plan, and The *Internet Start-Up Bible* is an ideal foundation on which to build your bridge. Success in the online world requires both planning and passion. This book offers plenty of both. The only other ingredient you need is some good luck – and your own personal karma will have to provide that.

The potential rewards of success in the European online world are great. Viewed from the United States, Europe is an awakening giant. A recent report from Forrester on the potential of Europe offers a few facts about business drivers that make this book so timely:

★ EU countries, plus Norway and Switzerland, make up the largest trading bloc in the world, with over 386 million consumers. That's 27% larger than the US and Canada combined.
★ In 1999, internet penetration at home doubled to cover 49 million people – 13% of the population. Some 20% of Europe's consumers use the web at work, and we can expect that over 200 million

European consumers will have web access by 2004.

★ Europe's B2B and B2C e-commerce will grow at triple digit rates, creating a $1.6 trillion market in the next five years. And that is still only 6.3% of the continent's total trade, leaving plenty of room for future growth.

★ By 2004, e-commerce in Europe will grow to more than 50% the size of the US e-commerce market.

And if those numbers are not enough to convince you that the upside potential for internet investments is huge, consider that AOL's recent $350 billion acquisition of Time-Warner is equivalent to the GDP of India ($357.4 billion), the fifteenth highest in the world. It is also more than the 1997 industrial output of the UK ($316 billion), which is the seventh highest in the world.

This dramatic growth in the value of e-commerce is being driven by increasingly inexpensive (or even free) internet access, plus unheard-of access to capital, both in Europe and the US.

The internet gives the would-be entrepreneur instant access to this fast-growing market of consumers and information, and this book gives the reader access to a wealth of invaluable information on how to exploit it. Researched in depth by an experienced team, this book lets you learn from other entrepreneurs' mistakes, as well as from some spectacular successes. It pulls together information and insights it would take you months to track down yourself. It is also written in a style that is easy to read – which is most important, because as an internet entrepreneur the only real barriers to success will be access to human capital, and leveraging your most valuable resource: intellectual bandwidth – your time.

So before you leap into the fray, pay heed to Sun Tzu and make sure you cannot lose before you try to win. Take a breath. Pause to plan. Read this book. It will help you build a bridge to get your business across that gulf filled with good ideas which are badly executed. On the other side is a new economy full of rich and rewarding opportunities.

Clive Pinder
Client Partner, Viant

Preface

As management consultants, we help companies develop and implement growth strategies by launching new products, entering new markets, and making acquisitions. We also work for private equity firms and venture capitalists, helping them to assess potential investments.

We have been investigating the threats and opportunities presented by the internet since 1995, when we started looking at the prospects for online classified advertising for a major client. In the half-decade since then we have reviewed a large number of businesses which depend (or will depend) on the internet for their existence. We have watched with fascination as the internet has progressed from being a clunky toy to being an essential business tool.

In December 1999 we ran a survey among executives in the private equity community. One of the findings was that investors are receiving literally hundreds of business plans a day, but many of them are poorly written, incomplete, or lacking in business insight.

Hence this book.

No book of this sort can ever be comprehensive – or perhaps even finished. Our optimistic publisher at Random House tells us there will be many reprints, so if you spot any errors or omissions, please write, and we will try to include them in later editions.

And a final word to those of you who really are going to quit your day jobs and start an Internet business: Keep healthy, work hard, and be lucky!

Calum Chace
Tess Read
Simon Rowe
London, San Francisco and Montserrat, February 2000

Acknowledgements

T he experience and understanding to write this book were gleaned from discussions with numerous people over the past few years. Some entrepreneurs and advisers have wished to remain anonymous, but we are keen to thank the following people who have made direct and very useful contributions (they cannot, of course, be blamed for any of the book's shortcomings): Riccardo Abbate (Withers), Jeremy Andrews (Greig Middleton), Azeem Azhar (eSouk.com), Lyn Barcow (Withers) Martin Beake, Maxine Benson (everywoman.co.uk), Robert Bond (Hobson Audley), Neil Brazil (Stock Exchange), Caraline Brown (Midnight Communications), Martin Cheesborough (Quidnunc), Richard Cienciala, Judith Clegg (moonfruit.com), Glen Collins (Digital-outlook), Neil Crofts (Razorfish), Simon Darling, Daniel Davies (Robert Fleming), Alan Dawson (Ernst & Young), Richard Downs (iglu.com), Mark Ellis (Redwood New Media), Chris Frost (onseniors.com), Ian Gardiner (lastorders.com), Dan Geoghegan (HMV), Paul Gill (aloud.com), Nick Hadlow, Tracey Harper (AMR), Simon Havers (ABN Amro), Christina Hemsley (A. T. Kearney), John Hemsley (isnit), Rob Hersov (Sportal), Sarah Hill (Inland Revenue), Mark Holmes (space2.com), Jeremy Hughes (Stock Exchange), Liat Joshi (AMR), Emma Kane (Redleaf Communications), Susan Kish (First Tuesday), Rupert Lee-Browne (eggsbenefit.com), Sonia Lo (ezoka.com), Richard Lord (*Revolution*), Charles Losa (AMR), Anne McCreary (Fresh Communications), Charles Meaden (Digital Nation), Jane Peel (AMR), Jeff and Kim Pinsker (for allowing Calum to monopolise their computer while supposedly on holiday), Ferdinand Porak (Deutsche Kleinwort Benson), Robert Postlethwaite (capitalstrategies.co.uk), Michael Ross (easyshop.com), David Rothschild, Anna Russell (silicon.com), Tony Ryan (Deloitte Touche), Clive Savage (Fletcher Research), Kevin Sefton (Y-creds), Mike Shaw (Fletcher Research), Chris Sheffield (Eunite), Peter Smail (NatWest), Rob Smeddle (Client Logic), Graham Stevens (Hyperlink), Rohit Taiway (Fast Future Ventures), Paul Vickery (3i), Julian Walker (Citigate Dewe Rogerson) – and, of course, our publisher, Clare Smith.

Introduction

'In five years' time all companies will be internet companies or
they will not be companies at all.'

ANDY GROVE, INTEL

'People always overestimate the impact that
new technologies will have in the short term,
and underestimate their long-term impact.'

ALVIN TOFFLER, AUTHOR OF *FUTURE SHOCK*
AND *THE THIRD WAVE*

The internet and e-commerce: hype or revolution?

Since the arrival of the World Wide Web in 1994 brought it to public attention, the internet has been subject to swings of hype and backlash. The current buzzword is e-business, and we are in the midst of the hype phase. The backlash is sure to follow, but neither the hype nor the backlash will tell the whole story. E-business is here to stay; it is already bringing about major changes to business life, and more will follow.

What is e-business, and does it matter?

E-commerce means selling products and services online, and e-business is taking that process further and making the entire company 'web-enabled', so that employees, suppliers, environmentalists, regulators, investors, everybody can carry out online whatever transaction they want to make. Is it going to have a big impact? Yes, because transacting online offers enormous benefits:

★ customers, suppliers, investors, etc. can be addressed as individuals, not as averages (this is known as 'narrowcasting', an old-fashioned but useful term);

★ customers can respond immediately to an offer (and suppliers can respond immediately to a request, etc.) thanks to the internet's interactivity;

★ they can ask questions, and remove any obstacles to a transaction themselves;

★ they can use powerful search engines to identify and specify exactly the product, service or information they require;

★ the only limits to what can be presented are your time and imagination – for example, music and book retailers can present enormous back-catalogues which offline stores could never hope to do;

★ customers and other stakeholders do not have to live near, or travel to, an outlet to see for themselves what is in it.

Although predictions are difficult and often doomed to failure we are prepared to stick our necks out and forecast that e-commerce and e-business will grow very fast because they offer major benefits to customers. Beware both 'e-vangelists' and doom-sayers; e-commerce will bring neither perfect democracy nor the totalitarian state. It will not create perfect markets where price is the only factor. We believe that widespread dis-intermediation which many have predicted, whereby middle-men are cut out of transactions, is unlikely. And contrary to what many have said, we consider that brands will become more important online, not less.

Perhaps the most fundamental, and the most interesting question about e-business is whether it represents a totally new way of doing business, or whether the net is simply another medium to sit alongside the phone, the fax, letters and so on.

The answer, of course, is somewhere between the two. In one sense the Andy Grove claim at the start of this chapter that all companies must become internet companies is correct. But that does not mean that the old rules of business just flew out of the window, and that all the familiar names in the FT500 are about to disappear and be replaced by cars.com, clothes.com and consultancy.com.

Just another new medium, or the medium to end all media?

Our view is that the internet will not destroy its predecessors, such as newspapers, telephones, cinema, radio and TV. Several of these innovations were expected to destroy their predecessors, but in fact they all survived, and in some cases thrived, after initial turbulence. The internet may evolve into a transmission channel for its predecessors, but for the foreseeable future, newspapers, cinema, radio and TV will persist in recognisable forms.

E-books and e-newspapers may replace paper some time in the next couple of decades, if the remarkable light-reflecting properties of paper can be reproduced and surpassed by screen technology. But reading is the most efficient means of communicating some types of information, and publishers, editors and journalists will still be needed to generate, assemble and edit what we read.

For a great many years to come, people will still gather together to experience what the latest screen-based entertainment can offer. It may involve elements of virtual reality (as in 'the feelies' in Huxley's *Brave New World*), but it will not be unrecognisable to cinema-goers of the past.

People will still want to listen to music and conversation while they are on the move, or pottering around their houses. It may be delivered over the internet, but it will be recognisably radio.

The internet changes fast

Change in the online world is fast and furious. The leading internet companies are concluding significant partnership deals every single day. They are experimenting and changing, too. They are partnering with competitor A one week, and replacing them with competitor B the next week.

Business models change fast too. Microsoft launched a free web-based magazine and was so encouraged by the response that it started to charge its readers. This proved unpopular, so they removed the charge. Offline, that sort of chopping and changing would spell disaster; online, everything is up for grabs.

CHAPTER 1

You

'Being an entrepreneur is years of taking a paycut and meeting people at Starbucks, not at a posh conference hall . . . and not being able to buy that suit that you want.'

SONIA LO, FOUNDER OF EZOKA.COM

'At the very outset, I was determined to deserve success.'

P.T. BARNUM

'So long as I am in control, I have a stake in whether I'm right or wrong.'

AN WANG, DESIGNER OF THE CALCULATOR AND FOUNDER OF WANG

What does it take to be an entrepreneur?

The first question you have to ask yourself is: are you an entrepreneur? To set up a successful business you will need almost inexhaustible supplies of vision, drive and coffee. History shows us that successful entrepreneurs share particular characteristics; few of the most famous were or are what you would call ordinary people.

Entrepreneurs are, above all, **sellers**, salespeople at heart

The gift of the gab, charisma, call it what you will, entrepreneurs have it. You may not always like them, but you're taken in by them and, crucially, so is everyone else. Why is this characteristic so vital? Because if you are going to start up and run a business, you are going to have to be someone who can sell your ideas to others, sell yourself and your team to the venture capitalists (VCs), and then sell your product or service to customers.

One characteristic of being good at selling yourself is being prepared to tackle everything and anything. Richard Branson particularly exemplifies this. He has never been known to be scared of huge established companies, because he realises that whatever the situation, everything is up for grabs. As one person has said of him: 'The way he sees it with Virgin Atlantic and Virgin Cola is that if he takes on the big boys and loses, he is a hero for trying. And if he wins, he is a genius.'

'I quite like having the ability to go and shake up the travel industry. It's fun.'

MARTHA LANE FOX,
CO-FOUNDER OF
LASTMINUTE.COM

Entrepreneurs are **risk-takers**

Many of the successful ones go broke several times before, and even after, making it. The principle here is not merely that they are prepared to risk bankruptcy but more that they welcome risk, they seek it, so making a fortune and then just sticking with it is not enough – they want to go on to try new and bigger ventures. A classic example of this is Rupert Murdoch, who took a huge risk launching Sky, a risk that could have taken down his other business ventures had it failed.

But the risks are calculated. Successful entrepreneurs are good judges of acceptable risk levels. They research a topic before trying to make decisions. They tend to be an adventurous group but minimise their risk with alternative plans should something unexpected arise. Starting a business is inherently risky, so you must research and plan before jumping in with both feet:

'Did I want to risk an embarrassing and costly failure? Absolutely.'

MICHAEL BLOOMBERG, FOUNDER OF BLOOMBERG

Entrepreneurs are **driven**

For what? For success, leading to money. This is the right way round, because otherwise you're likely to be too impatient to get the money and then too eager to spend it when you get it. Journalists who visit the corporate headquarters of amazon.com are amazed to see the scruffy corridors and plastic coffee cups. Jeff Bezos disarmingly explains that the lack of mahogany means that every spare penny (not that it's profit yet, of course, but anyway) goes into better infrastructure, more and better staff, making the company grow and prosper:

'Gates is tenacious, he keeps coming at you. That's what's scary. He's like Chinese water torture.'

EDITOR OF *BUSINESS WEEK*, ON BILL GATES

We have a strong focus on trying to spend money on things that matter to customers and not spend money on us. Instead, we spend money on things that matter to customers, like having the best servers, having the best T3 lines, having the best people, because our people really matter to our customers. Those things count, but almost nothing else does.

This also means personal as well as corporate privations. Why do entrepreneurs do this? Because they are, as Warren Avis, the founder of Avis, says, 'monomaniacs' – one-track-minded obsessives capable of putting one thing, success, ahead of everything else. And they are this way because something has made them so. Examples abound of destitute boys from the Warsaw ghetto who made good in America, such as Samuel Goldwyn, but also of more parochial cases of people who are damaged in some way by a parent walking out on them when they were three years old.

A vital corollary of being driven is having staying power. The law of timing is that everything will always take longer than you expect, and the law of new ventures is that something will always go wrong. But entrepreneurs keep ploughing on and on, because they have something to prove to themselves, and to others. The founders of student-net.co.uk, which sold a 74% stake to International Media Products of Nevada for £10 million, explained their success: 'It's all about persistence. We worked twenty-four hours a day seven days a week for six months and every time a door closed on us we just kept trying other things until another one opened.'

'Do you feel it passionately, because that's the only thing that will drive it.'

MAXINE BENSON, CO-FOUNDER OF EVERYWOMAN

'You have to have something in you that keeps you going through the hundred times when everyone including a part of yourself thinks you should give up.'

RICHARD DUVALL, CHIEF EXECUTIVE OF EGG.COM

Entrepreneurs are also **very hard workers** – *very* hard workers

Chris Frost, founder of onseniors.com, agrees: 'Because of the hype people think that you go out there and put up a web site and then you are rich. But it's not like that. It's hard to get people to your site and it's more work than you can imagine. It's twelve hours a day, seven days a week and very little money.'

Not only does this mean you have to be prepared for *very* long hours for a *long* time, meaning that most entrepreneurs started out when they had an unencumbered private life, it also means you've probably got to love it and want to keep doing it. Retiring at forty with a shedload of cash is not usually the long-term aim of successful entrepreneurs.

As Jeff Bezos has said, 'I'm here for a long time. If there were a faster-changing place somewhere, maybe I would be tempted, but that doesn't seem likely. I can't imagine anything more fun to do.'

Entrepreneurs are generally thought of as **bold, brash people**

Why? Because in getting going they have usually had to be utterly shameless in asking friends and family for money and contacts, and doing the same to every person the widening network extends to.

Entrepreneurs **think big**

Part of the reason entrepreneurs use all possible contacts is not only to get going, but also because they think big. Stelios Haji-Ioannou, founder of Easyjet and Easyeverything, says: 'Businesses aren't worth starting unless they're going to be big – at least £100 million.' If you would be satisfied with making it medium, you'll never make it big. Virgin is a classic example: it was already big, but not totally massive in a hundred different areas. Branson saw a new challenge, creating a 'nomad brand' (see Marketing, chapter 7) and took it.

Entrepreneurs can **handle rejection**, again and again

Not only are entrepreneurs prepared to risk bankruptcy, they are also prepared for VCs etc. to tell them their idea is not up to it, or that the valuation of their company is more like £40 million than £100 million. The key is not just being able not to take it personally, but also to deal with it and carry on. Dealing with rejection is part of being an entrepreneur. Just trying to get a business started you are liable to run into opposition from friends, family, creditors, business associates and soon-to-be ex-colleagues. When you become an entrepreneur you step out of the comfort zone for many people. You have got to be prepared not only for failing, but for jealous people to want you to fail.

'Success breeds arrogance and complacency; adversity breeds strength. You will never be better than during the tough times. And while the tough times don't last, tough people do.'

ROSS PEROT

Entrepreneurs **take decisions easily and want to lead**

Successful entrepreneurs are people who take decisions easily and quickly. This character trait is usually part of a broader picture: entrepreneurs want to lead. They chafe under authority and escaping its grip is often a key part of why they wanted to set up their own company. This motivation often leads to a seriously ruthless streak. One famous anecdote about Robert Maxwell has him firing someone by mobile phone in the time it took this person to walk from the wrong door of the Ritz Hotel, where he was waiting for Maxwell, to the door Maxwell claimed he had specified.

'One of the first things a man has to learn in business is how little he can do by himself. When he finds that out he begins to look around for people to do what he can't.'

HENRY FORD

But leadership does not mean completing every task yourself, and successful entrepreneurs should know how to delegate. One of the keys to success in entrepreneurship is the ability to choose others who you trust and then delegate work to them. When you are starting up a new business you cannot possibly know how to do everything yourself – even if you did, you don't have the time to do everything yourself. Delegate those tasks you do not know how to do and concentrate on the areas in which you excel.

'The first thing you have to learn as an entrepreneur is to admit your ignorance – you must learn you cannot do everything by yourself.'

SONIA LO, FOUNDER OF EZOKA.COM

In fact, because of their wish to be in charge, many entrepreneurs fail to delegate enough and try to do everything themselves. This always leads them to work triply hard, and usually leads to a Damascene conversion. Warren Avis comments: 'I've started to concentrate more on hiring top managers . . . to take over when I decide to go on to new ventures. My guess is that I would be worth a hundred times more money if I had just learned to do this years ago.'

Entrepreneurs **innovate**

Entrepreneurs are not necessarily school-clever; indeed, many of them performed badly at school (Branson again!), but they innovate and are interested in innovating, and will not stick for ever with a company they have set up, but after it's truly up and running will move on to another, and another. Apart from anything else, there are different skills involved in having an idea for a company and setting it up, and then running it as an ongoing business.

Entrepreneurs can **solve problems**

Entrepreneurs have an uncanny ability to find solutions for difficult problems. The business environment of a start-up company will present you with many unique problems. How do you approach a problem? Are you prepared to spend time analysing it and finding a solution – not analysis leading to paralysis, but neither shutting your eyes and hoping for the best?

Entrepreneurs also have an **attention to detail**

You have to be prepared to deal not only with ideas, but with the facts of your business too. Often there may be no one around to deal with the small things but you, such as dealing with the fire officer who demands an unannounced inspection, or arguing with your telephone company when they fail you miserably again. The reason there may be no one around is that no one will care as much about your business as you – or at least no one should.

Entrepreneurs are **flexible**

This is an essential skill for entrepreneurs. Do you accept new ideas easily? Treat other people's ideas with respect? Are you able to make decisions right away? An entrepreneur must be open-minded, flexible and able to respond to new ideas.

Entrepreneurs are willing to **learn new skills**

A classic example showing why this is crucial is that although you may not think you have a head for numbers, if you are to run a successful business you are going to have to learn to analyse data such as web traffic, and indeed balance sheets, showing you where you are spending your money. You may think you can delegate this to an accountant you trust, and certainly they can calculate the figures, but you must interpret them so that you can respond correctly and quickly.

Internet entrepreneurs have to be doubly flexible, because their world turns upside down every month or so. Richard Duvall, chief executive of egg.com, says: 'Every two months we find we have to throw away the plans and start all over again, because everything has changed.'

Entrepreneurs are **optimists**

They have to be. Sometimes their ideas are useless, and if they're not enthusiastic and optimistic about them, no one else will be.

How suited are you to entering the particular business area you intend to enter?

Do you have the right knowledge? You will need to know a reasonable amount about your business area to begin with, in order to build on it. Indeed, the business area you enter should have been an interest of yours for some time.

Is there a skill set or contact set which is vital for the business? For example, it is doubtful that boo.com would have made such a splash if Kajsa Leander had not been a model. Most successful entrepreneurs can be put into one of the following categories; so should you.

★ **Talented** at a particular skill – e.g. a whiz-kid, a cyber superstar. Beware: there are lots of people who think they are the next potential Bill Gates. If this is your forte, chances are you're not necessarily suited to being a people-person entrepreneur, in which case you would be better off partnering up with people who are. The only other alternative is just to sell the idea to someone who can take it forward.
★ **A networker** – potentially the ideal type of person to go

'I had the entrepreneurial desire to set up a new company and to do it in a sport that I enjoy.'

RICHARD DOWNS, CO-FOUNDER, IGLU.COM

about getting the people and funding together to start up a business, providing you can knuckle down to desk-based work too. Even so, this may not be quite the right kind of person to run and manage the business.

★ **A motivator** will act as a catalyst, bringing people's talents and motivation to the fore, which is ideal for the gruelling, hard-working days of starting a business, and indeed can be the ideal type of person to run a business. A motivating person can make a good manager; a de-motivating person can only ever make a bad manager. A motivator doesn't necessarily mean someone who is showy and leads the singing in a company song he or she wrote, it can just mean someone who notices others' talents, ideas and concerns and can successfully encourage.

★ **A visionary**. All entrepreneurs are visionary to some extent in that they see a possibility which no one has attempted, or possibly even seen, before. But this doesn't mean you have to be Edison or Bell or Gates to succeed. Of course, if you are, that's good, but it's unlikely.

CHAPTER 2

Idea

Reproduced by the kind permission of BVCA

'If you're going to succeed, you need a vision, one that's affordable, practical, and fills a customer need. Then, go for it. Don't worry too much about the details.'

MICHAEL BLOOMBERG, FOUNDER OF BLOOMBERG

'There are some people of course who say that opportunity went out with the horse and buggy. That's rubbish . . . There is always a better way of doing almost everything.'

CLARENCE BIRDSEYE, FOUNDER OF BIRDSEYE AND INVENTOR OF THE METHOD FOR MASS QUICK FREEZING

'Making a fortune is not easy at all. The first thing you need is an inspirational idea. . . . Is it easy to paint a great painting or compose a symphony? It's not.'

TOM TEICHMANN, NEW MEDIA INVESTORS

Introduction

So you have an idea for an internet business, but how good an idea is it? Before you write a business plan to try to raise funding for your business, and before you even start to research formally the precise mechanics of how the business will work, you should sit down and assess the idea. Take it from the 'back of an envelope' stage to a few pages of A4 on the basis of your own knowledge and that of a few trusted, and preferably knowledgeable, confidantes.

The key areas you are attempting to address in evaluating your idea are:

★ Who are the customers for your product/service?
★ Will they want to buy your product/service?
★ Who will you be competing with for their business?
★ What will make you different?
★ What will make you attractive to customers and so win their business?

'A business is a business is a business. Just because it's on the web doesn't mean that somehow the normal rules of finding a market and running a business don't apply. They do – it's just that it's a new medium and new media open up new fields of business, and these are always wide open for newcomers in the beginning.'

INTERNET
CONSULTANT

'Show me the money'

From reading the newspapers you could gain the idea that internet businesses never have to make profits. Wrong. Your business plan should be clear about how your idea will make money. According to Paul Vickery from 3i, the biggest venture capital provider in Europe, 'I have seen a number of plans which make almost no mention of where actual revenue is going to come from. When asked where the business is actually going to get its money from the answer is always, "Oh, from advertising." This is an extremely unattractive proposition.'

Relying on advertising is risky

The internet is no longer so new that there are only a few sites with advertisers clamouring to get on to them. You can only generate serious amounts of revenue if you are someone like Yahoo! Elsewhere advertising rates are falling, largely because advertising on the net has not proved a great success so far (see Marketing, chapter 7). But the issue here is wider than this, in that for most businesses there should be several sources of revenue.

As Ferdinand Porak from Dresdner Kleinwort Benson's venture capital unit says, 'One thing I am particularly looking for in a business proposal is multiple revenue streams.'

What makes money online?

For almost any industry the internet offers the potential to reap cost efficiencies, sometimes huge efficiencies. Unless you are offering a product/service online, which does not currently exist offline, your business idea will be aiming to capitalise on these efficiencies to make money, and beat the offline competition in doing so. So in crystallising your business idea you need to locate it precisely within its market and work out exactly what problems or inefficiencies you will be solving. When thinking about this you may find

'The internet offers the opportunity to revolutionise supply chains.'

DAN GEOGHEGAN,
ONLINE STRATEGIST
AT HMV

your initial conception of your potential customers changes, as you realise you can boil down the supply chain more and more. One way of thinking about this is to imagine yourself as a customer in this industry and work out exactly what you would ideally want from a provider.

The 'killer application'

In addition to the different ways in which businesses will make money from offering goods versus services online, as the internet has grown it has become clear that having a 'killer application' is the key to attracting visitors because all sites are equally convenient, unlike in the traditional high street. This means that your site has to be associated with the provision of one thing which is very important or useful or attractive to customers, whatever that may be. The idea is to get customers to associate your site with everything to do with that area.

Amazon.com was set up to sell books, and specifically to sell all books still in print. This means that its competitive positioning was that it would provide a comprehensive selection of books which would be more than any offline shop could offer. One fashionable way of thinking about this is that the business is 'an inch wide and a mile deep'.

While Amazon provides a clear example of how this is achievable in the world of goods, Chemdex E, a chemical trading site, is an example from the world of services. This is what is known as a 'vertically integrated portal', or 'vortal', which aims to provide people with everything to do with a particular industry and also aims to perform another function at which the internet excels: creating communities of people linked online, and then potentially offline, by a common interest.

Hortals versus vortals

However, other internet businesses favour the horizontal portal (or 'hortal') approach. These aim to capture a horizontal slice of a market or economy. Sites for women such as handbag.com and charlottestreet.com are classic examples. These sites believe they can make money by offering a wide variety of goods and services, although some observers believe that if a hortal does not have a clear enough identity, users will go straight to the providers of the actual services.

Some online companies claim to offer the attractions of both hortals and vortals. For example, Andrew Doe, co-founder of confetti.co.uk, a wedding portal that offers wedding-related information and services, claims 'we're going to be very wide and very deep'.

'There are too many websites that are too broad and too shallow – they won't survive.'

MAXINE BENSON, CO-FOUNDER OF EVERYWOMAN.COM

Infrastructure versus content

The first distinctions to make in your mind are between offering internet infrastructure or using the web as merely a potentially cost-efficient medium for your business, or using the web as the only possible way to deliver your product/service.

Internet infrastructure

If you are intending to build or market internet infrastructure or internet-enabling technology, the good news is that history would suggest that on the wave of a trend this is a potentially very rich vein – as the adage runs, the people who made the most money from the gold rush in America were the people who sold the shovels to the fortune hunters.

The bad news is that the competition is stiff, and large players such as the all-powerful Microsoft heavily dominate the market. You face extreme competition for hiring staff from the thousands of offline businesses wanting to get online as well as from other start-ups like yourself. Web consultants are being hired for salaries upwards of £50,000 a year plus substantial share options, or for around £1,000 a day. Mark Hughes, the UK managing director of BroadVision, says, 'We hold our breath when we go into interviews now, wondering what people are going to ask for.'

Of course, hiring technology staff will be an issue for any online business, but will be of particularly great concern for internet infrastructure businesses.

The internet is the medium

Most web businesses use the internet purely as a medium for their business, a medium that can generate substantial cost savings compared with online businesses. Examples here include amazon.com, and CDnow.com. Many people argue that selling ideas/services is safer than selling things because the online retail market is likely to consolidate around a few mega brands while the knowledge market will continue to grow and diversify. 'Music, information and financial services are all very suitable because there are no delivery costs,' according to Benjamin Ensor of Fletcher Research. Goods that consumers have no particular desire to touch or handle prior to purchase that have proved popular.

Beware: a major issue for a web business selling things to consumers is the difficulty of delivery. Part of the success of sites selling CDs and books is that these products usually fit through letter-boxes. If your product won't, until some mechanism is sorted out for enabling products to be held at sensibly local and secure locations for customers, you will have to work hard to make your overall proposal to the customer more attractive than those of offline retailers.

The internet enables the product/service

It may be that the web provides the only possible way of delivering your business, such as is the case for lastminute.com. If so, you are likely to face similar technological issues as businesses that are creating internet infrastructure.

What is the market?

B2B or not B2B

Who are you going to be selling your product to? Is it business-to-business (B2B) product/service, or business-to-consumer (B2C)?

A B2C product/service will usually need to be a high-volume, low-price product. In any market at any time this is

'The vast marketing campaign that is necessary to make a B2C work is one reason I am sceptical of B2Cs, because consumer trends are highly volatile: people's tastes might change, and then it's just money burned.'

FERDINAND PORAK,
DRESDNER
KLEINWORT BENSON

potentially difficult for a new entrant, because of the low gross margins under which you would need to operate and because the huge marketing campaign you would have to launch would use up your seed capital very quickly. However, the internet offers an exceptional opportunity to cut costs compared with established suppliers – *if*, that is, they have not already entered the market, which by now they probably have. An alternative customer attraction in a B2C business is extraordinarily personalised customer focus, i.e. offering the same product/service as the established players, but doing it better.

Some B2B product/services have huge customer bases (like the software from Oracle), but B2B companies generally raise substantially more revenue per customer and therefore a B2B business can survive with fewer customers, certainly in the growing stages. Moreover, most online start-up B2Bs (and, indeed, offline start-up B2B businesses) are created by people who have previously worked in that industry, and a significant part of their business model consists of bringing their contacts (who will be their customers) with them. Most commentators are expecting B2B e-commerce greatly to outstrip B2C in revenue terms.

Who will your customers be, and what do they need or want?

When you carry out a formalised research process you will need to specify quite precisely the characteristics of your target customer base. At this initial stage you should try to isolate the broad target group and think around the likely characteristics of this group.

In any business it is essential to know who your

customers are and what their characteristics are. Think about opening a restaurant or a bar. Different bars clearly have different atmospheres and offerings, designed to appeal to different sorts of people – young, old, trendy, rich, poor. It is similar for the customers of any business: you need to be able to describe them closely – their likes and dislikes, where they shop, their age, income bracket. Of course, you may be wrong about who you will in fact appeal to (as smile.co.uk was – see Marketing, chapter 7), but you still have to try.

Working out who your customers are critically affects what marketing strategy to use – ranking on search engines is probably not helpful if you are appealing to CEOs or directors, as they probably won't be surfing the net. It also enables you to define the need that you are fulfilling. It may not always be obvious. For example, do customers really want to save the one pound Easyjet offers off its tickets when bought over the internet, or do they like it because using the internet lets them book tickets on the office computer rather than the home telephone, or because they want to 'join the new age', be trendy and book through the internet?

There is still a huge amount of room for innovation and improvement and making customers' lives better. This is still day one, in terms of what you can create online.'

JEFF BEZOS, FOUNDER
OF AMAZON.COM

What is your business strategy?

You need to work out what your business strategy is, and identify the various strategies adopted by your competition. It has been argued that there are seven possible business strategies:

1. **High end**. This is a business that combines an 'upmarket' image and features that come to be regarded as commodities in and of themselves, such as a brand name which is a byword for luxury, such as Harrods or Chanel. This strategy tries to persuade customers that to buy from Harrods is to make a statement about themselves.

2. **No frills**. This business approach is right at the other end of the scale, epitomised by the 'pile it high, sell it cheap' motto once used by Tesco and now adopted by Walmart. The emphasis here is on basic functionality. Low-cost airlines such as Easyjet and Go are classic examples. Even though Easyjet may have a trendy web site and Stelios Haji-Ioannou puts good jokes about BA's losses on it, there is no escaping the fact that no food is served on the flights and the stewards and stewardesses do not wear the fancy uniforms of Singapore Airlines. This, then, becomes a badge of pride for their customers and feeds back into the perception of the business, and reinforces the brand.

3. **One-stop shopping**. There are two opposing forces operating on any business: to diversify or to remain a niche player. At the beginning you have no choice; you have to choose a niche, a killer application, and with success and luck you may be able to expand from there, as Amazon is doing and as Virgin seems to specialise in doing.

4. **Superior performance**. You may be able to offer better functionality than established online businesses. For example, the fastest web search engine currently seems to be alltheweb.com. But not all customers will be prepared to pay extra for superior performance.

5. **Superior customer support**. The internet offers the potential to serve customers better by enabling quick,

easy ordering. Moreover, clever web site add-ons enable cheap instant access to the exact department they need to contact. But web businesses also have the potential to offer customers worse customer support than offline businesses. The difficulties of delivering large goods to B2C consumers are just one example.

6. **Customer involvement**. The web offers the opportunity to involve customers in the purchasing process by customising sites. This has proved to be an effective strategy for online businesses such as Amazon. But it is questionable whether this approach alone would be a sufficient attraction to wean people away from offline businesses.

7. **Affinity branding**. Some customers may be interested in banking with the bank that David Bowie endorses. They may choose to ignore other factors such as the price and performance of the service.

Who's afraid of the competition?

Whatever your market, you are likely to face competition. This can be in the form of businesses offering your product, or those offering a substitute for your product, and may be in the form of:

★ offline businesses ('bricks and mortar' businesses);
★ offline businesses going online ('clicks and mortar' businesses);
★ online businesses;

★ online businesses based in other countries which may move here (the US is the biggest likely source of such competitors);

★ rival start-ups.

At first, when you consider the competition you may fear that it is too strong for you to be able to compete. Of course this could be true, and certain markets are believed by most to be sewn up (such as the online market for books, for example). But there may be a way for your business to make money in even quite a mature market, by finding a niche. Niches are small parts of a market, large enough to enable you to make lots of money but small enough for a start-up to be a big fish in a small pond. But niches may well not be what you are interested in. After all, the whole point of the internet is that it enables small businesses to get very big very fast.

Mature markets

If you are entering a mature market you may be able to find ways in which the current players are out of step with the consumer:

★ the customer's needs have moved on, but the supplier has not noticed;

★ you have spotted a better way of doing things and can introduce it to customers.

A good example of a mature market is that for beer in the UK. Sales have been gently declining for years, but the market is still worth £7 billion a year. Lastorders.com, a web site selling beer, believes that if it can take a modest portion of that market by offering a combination of low prices, convenience and choice, then it can create a valuable business.

Look, no competition

Some online businesses do not initially face competition because they are based on an idea that can't be replicated offline. Rather than replicating an offline business on the internet, these companies have spotted a new way in which the web can be used (or, more likely, have spotted a US web company using the technique). Some companies, such as LetsBuyIt.com, are based on the ability to aggregate customer orders and use the greater bargaining power to negotiate lower prices than the individual customers would be able to achieve. Other companies, such as lastminute.com, use the internet's ability to collect, process and sift information at speed.

Some of the specialist auction sites are allowing buyers and sellers to come together to haggle over products such as second-hand power stations that they previously did not know were available. All these kinds of businesses would not be possible without the web. Of course, in any of these areas competitors are likely to spring up, but there may be a period of grace in which to establish first-mover advantage.

'The really cool thing is when someone comes up with an idea that just can't operate anywhere else but the web – like lastminute.com.'

NIELS BRYAN-LOW, PROTEUS

'We were originally thinking of a "bricks and mortar" business, but that changed when we saw some of the US web sites aimed at women. There was nothing similar available in the UK.'

MAXINE BENSON, CO-FOUNDER OF EVERYWOMAN

What is your competitive strategy?

Once you have considered your competition, you need to think about how you are going to deal with them. Liam Fahey, author of the book *Competitors*, has isolated four mechanisms:

1. **Frontal**. This means taking on an established online player with an equivalent product or service targeted at the same customer group. This is a brave, although not necessarily unwise, strategy, depending on whether you truly have a USP (unique selling proposition; see Plan, Chapter 3) that would enable you to succeed.
2. **Flanking**. This means entering a defined market, well mapped out by established players, but with a modified product or targeting a different customer set.
3. **Bypass by innovating**. The new world of the internet opens up a panoply of business opportunities which involve out-flanking established players (especially offline, but online too) by innovating because the internet has brought and will continue to bring 'discontinuities' into markets – opportunities to redesign the supply chain and thereby cut costs or improve service. Established players who have built up success offline may instinctively see these discontinuities as threats, but you can see them as opportunities.
4. **Encirclement**. This entails setting out a broader product/service than anyone in the competition (for example, in books or CDs) and going after a wider array of customers.

Business prospects

You now have the building blocks to work out the prospects for your business. There are two factors which determine these prospects: the prospects for the market, and the prospects for your particular business. As you consider these, you should build up an initial SWOT – Strengths, Weaknesses, Opportunities and Threats – for your business:

Possible strengths

★ attractive new way for customers to buy product/ service xyz;
★ strong, experienced management team with all necessary skills;
★ support from key technology partners.

Possible weaknesses

★ no brand recognition;
★ no office yet.

Opportunities

★ business model is innovative and not fully tested in practice;
★ huge market growth expected by all pundits.

Threats (and mitigants)

★ low barriers to competitive entry (high marketing spend planned to capitalise on first-move advantage);

★ collapse in high-tech stocks devalues your company paper (but cash to be raised in this 'financing round' – see Funding, chapter 6 – will suffice for one year's development).

Determining Business Prospects

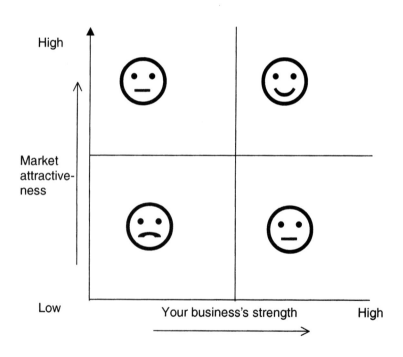

Checklist

This is a checklist of questions for you to consider and talk over with your co-conspirators, and maybe a couple of trusted friends. You should have positive answers to most of them before going on to the next stage of formulating an initial business plan.

1. Will people want to buy what you are offering?
2. Is your product/service suitable to be sold online?
3. Will customers be willing to pay enough for you to be able to make money, given your costs in selling the product/service?
4. Is there someone already providing your product/service, or an acceptable substitute for it?
5. How will you beat them?
6. Are there high barriers to entry?
7. Can you erect barriers once you have entered?
8. What kinds of people do you need to run your company, and sell your product?
9. Are you willing to do what it takes to set up your business?
10. Do you have a USP?

CHAPTER 3
Plan

Reproduced by the kind permission of BVCA

'We see some really dull me-too business plans, with no partnerships and no drawing on the resources of the old world. We also see some really good people attached to some truly terrible business plans.'

STEWART DODDS, BRAINSPARK

What is a business plan?

The business plan for your business sets out:

★ what your business idea is;
★ who the key people are on your team who will implement the idea;
★ what your financial forecasts are for your business;
★ why your company will beat the competition;
★ how your idea will be executed;
★ how much money you are asking from the funder to whom you are taking this idea.

Why write a business plan?

Few people would say that writing a business plan is a particularly enjoyable thing to do, but it is absolutely essential, because a business plan sets out the fundamentals of your business in a formal and clear way to:

★ yourself;
★ potential funders;
★ potential staff;
★ other potential partners.

Without a business plan you cannot hope to attract professional (venture capital or angel) money, nor can you demonstrate to others that you have a realistic business venture which they should join. Writing a plan it is also an excellent way to demonstrate to yourself that you are serious. Almost as important, it is an excellent way to challenge your own thinking and force yourself to be thorough in your analysis and your research.

Write it *now!*

The way to generate a business plan is to write down everything you know about the market for your product/service and then translate it into a themed, formally constructed document along the lines set out below. You may think you should not attempt to do a business plan before you have done your research, but there are three good reasons why you should not delay, and just begin:

1. You should consider your business plan to be 'iterative', which is to say a partial attempt at the subject which awaits further information and fine-tuning. This means that you can expect to revise fundamentally what you first set down in the light of later research so that the business plan you eventually present to potential funders will have come a long way from your first attempt.
2. You *can* generate financial forecasts for your business, even before you have talked to potential distributors, let alone customers. How? By making assumptions. So at this stage you assume the cost of distribution, staff and office space, and assume the price that customers would be willing to pay for your product/service. Later on you can alter your financial forecasts, and possibly crucial elements of your business model, in the light of your research.
3. Writing a business plan is a chore, but it absolutely has to be done. If you find yourself putting off writing a

business plan you have to question whether you're serious about your business idea.

Finally, there is a lot of software to computer-generate your business plan, such as at dcfor.com and sbaonline.com. Do not be tempted! It does not take a particularly sharp VC to spot one, and when they do, your business plan will be turned into the next paper aeroplane.

What should the focus be?

Remember that in the final version the aim of your business plan is to raise money from funders; in the first version the aim of your business plan is to formalise your idea. In both cases what you are trying to isolate is how it will make money. Incredibly obvious, but, remarkably, often overlooked. 'I see so many internet start-up business plans which are full of stuff about the whizzy technology these kids have built and what it can do. I'm not interested – I want to know what the *business* idea is. I want to see how it's going to make money as a business' as one VC told us.

'Look at the business model. How much money are they going to piss away before they generate revenue and, in the end, make a profit?'

TOM TEICHMANN, NEW MEDIA INVESTORS

What style should the plan adopt?

In general, your business plan needs to strike a careful balance between realistic forecasts for what you can hope to achieve, and a 'sell' of your idea and your team. The best way to achieve this is to create for yourself an 'elevator pitch' (which is to say, a summary of your idea that can be explained in the time it takes you and your potential funder to ride up in the lift to his or her office) and to sell yourself and your team as a good proposition, but make sure your plan is a realistic assessment of the prospects for the market and your business.

In terms of writing style your business plan needs to be clear and easy to read; the target of your finished business plan is funders above all. They are very busy people, and a trait common to busy people is an increasing inability to process large text documents. Thus they progress from documents to executive summaries, until eventually a one-word bullet point is about their limit. While this is, of course, wild and no doubt unfair exaggeration, the point stands that it is important to present your idea simply and clearly. Only use jargon if necessary, and be sure to explain it.

There is no 'correct' length for a business plan, but what you present should be in proportion to the idea. If you are trying to raise £200,000 for a relatively simple proposition, then a tightly written document of ten pages will be plenty. But if your business will use complex technology and if you are trying to raise many millions of pounds, your document might run to 40 or 50 pages, with several appendices.

What should the plan contain?

Your business plan needs to tell your potential financiers about several things:

- ★ your business idea, i.e. your USP, or unique selling proposition;
- ★ the market;
- ★ the team;
- ★ the financial plan;
- ★ funding required.

Executive summary

More likely than not, this will be all you send to VCs in your initial contact with them, so make it short, snappy and good. Begin the summary with a one-sentence description of your business idea, the business name you have chosen, the name and positions of the key people involved and the highlights of your financial forecasts.

Follow this with a short paragraph on your USP (unique selling proposition). Your USP could come in many guises. You may believe (correctly or incorrectly) that you are the first to attempt a particular business idea for a certain sector, or you may have access to certain distribution/supply channels that will make your position more favourable than any competitor.

Then produce one or two paragraphs on each of the three remaining sections: the market, the team and the financial plan with the funding required. Top the executive summary with the title of your business and the domain name you intend to use, and tail it with contact details for yourself and your team.

Your executive summary is extremely important, so spend time crafting it and honing it. Although it fronts your plan, expect to write it after you have written the body of the plan.

Contents

Include a contents section only if your business plan is long enough to warrant it, and then make sure that the rest of it is professional enough to support it.

The business idea

Your business idea is your USP, the thing that makes you special. In describing your business idea you must identify what the definable customer need is, why your business is excellently placed to fill that need and how it will do so. In explaining your USP, you should make it clear why customers will want the new product/service you are supplying, or why you will beat the competition for an existing product/service.

Describe the form of your business idea and how and why it will make money. You need to answer the following questions:

★ What are you selling? Describe exactly what your product/service is and which industry it falls into. Is your business a B2C or a B2B? Are you using the internet as a medium or building internet infrastructure?

★ Are you offering a new product/service? If so, what makes you believe it is a wanted product/service, wanted enough for a sufficient number of people to pay for it?

★ Are you fulfilling a need you/others have recognised, or are you offering an established product/service but done better? If so, what is different about the product/service you are offering? In what ways precisely is it better? In what ways is it new?

You then need to consider how well your business is placed to fill that new need, or to offer an established product/service in a better way.

★ What are your key processes? You must determine what is essential about the running of your business. For any web business the technology is not just essential, it is a crucial aspect of the business (see Technology, chapter 9). Anyone considering funding an internet business will want to be assured that the people intending to implement the idea have a very clear idea of the technology needed and how it will be used. Having your technology issues sorted out means not only that you have to know what resources you need, but also that you have the key people on board. It is neither easy nor cheap to hire good technology people at the moment, for the obvious reason that they get so many offers (see People, chapter 10).

★ What are your expected supply sources? Do you have particularly good and stable relations with any suppliers, and are you dependent upon any? The question here is, do you have privileged supply relations, and if not, do you have disadvantaged supply relations?

★ What are your distribution channels? How do you intend to deliver your product? How will your delivery systems match up to or beat those of your competitors? 'I often see entrepreneurs who have come up with a great product, but they do not put forward a clear or easy way to sell it, nor do I see one,' said one VC.

The market

There are several things you need to show to funders about the market you intend to enter (which, of course, will need to be backed up by your research on the market). Here are the most common ones:

★ **Size**. You need to show the past growth and expected future growth for your market. VCs, in particular, are typically looking for high-growth markets to invest in. You may be able to raise funds against a plan to grab a significant share of a market which is growing more modestly.

★ **Segmentation**. Is your market fragmented with many small firms, or are there a few large organisations, selling a 'commodity' product between which consumers see no difference? Break down your customer base by geography, price sensitivity, quality requirements, etc.

★ **Dynamics**. What is changing in the market, and why? Perhaps, for example, a new competitor has entered the market with a new business model, and has caused a number of customers to switch suppliers.

Many would-be internet entrepreneurs think their product is so new that they do not have any direct competitors, but they are almost always wrong. Furthermore, even if you don't remember the lesson of Betamax versus VHS, your funders will. Your competitor can have a worse product than you, but it doesn't necessarily mean you will beat them. They may have a better management team, better marketing, a link with a key distributor, first-mover advantage, a better brand, greater financial strength, or tied-in customer loyalty. It is essential that you assess both your current competitors and your potential competitors against these criteria. You also need to know about potential online competitors outside the UK, both in Europe and in the US.

Simon Havers, a director of ABN Private Equity, says that it is very important to be honest about the competition in a business plan: 'Tell the whole truth. Be honest about the competition. If your competitors have key strengths that you fail to mention (or worse still, you fail to mention that the competitor exists at all) then, when the VC finds out (which 99% of the time he will), he will just decide you're either a liar or a poor manager who is incapable of basic market surveillance. Either way, you can forget any chance of getting funding from that VC.'

The team

VCs will set a great deal of store by who is behind the business and who will drive it forward. Ideally, you will have a number of your key posts filled by the time you approach a VC; if you do, you should include the CVs of each person, paying particular attention to their relevant business expertise. In general, the posts you need to fill to set up a web business are chief executive, sales director, IT director, finance director and chairman (see People, chapter 10, for details).

You should also describe your management plan for the company. How is it to be run? What is the legal form of your business: have you formed a limited company? How much capital has been invested so far, and how have you divided the equity stock? Show the organisational structure of the company and how it uses the skills of the people you have.

Be sure also to list anyone else you need, rather than pretend you are covering all essential posts. You will want to convince funders that you and your team are up to it and up for it, but beware the dangers of exaggeration.

Several VC sources say that with every *single* investment they make, they not only check out any references or exam results mentioned in CVs, they also hire private detectives to check out the private lives of the people involved. Not for any sinister purpose, but to check whether what people have said about their lives in general is true in order to work out whether they are generally trustworthy or not. It's not that VCs are trying to find out whether or not your mother was a Greenham Common activist, they are simply trying to discover whether you have lied or exaggerated in your CV, because if you have, this might suggest that your plans and financial forecasts for your business are exaggerations too.

The financial plan

You need numbers. Specifically, you need to produce forecast statements for profit and loss (P&L), balance sheets and cash flow. The purpose is to show how much money you will need to fund the business, where the business is going to make its money, and when it will produce profits. You may consider this irrelevant, given that internet companies are currently famous for their high valuations and losses, but such an analysis misses the point. Investors will commit funds to businesses they consider will make profits, substantial profits, at some point in the future. Admittedly, many dot.com companies floated on the Stock Exchange can be valued far more highly than is justified by their financial prospects, but VC investors will not be as irrational as day traders.

For a business that is already a going concern, VCs would expect to see financial forecasts for five or more years, but the rules are different for start-ups. At this stage, VCs will wish to see your financial forecasts in order to scrutinise the assumptions you have built into them, rather than to see what level of profits you expect to reach by the year 2020. In fact, including excessively detailed forecasts could damage your credibility, because everyone knows that at the start-up stage such forecasts are mere guesswork. Instead, you must assume your forecasts will change after weeks, and after months, but initial estimates must be included nonetheless.

It is a basic but important point that the numbers in the financial forecasts should be completely consistent with those in the text of the plan. VCs are quick to spot inconsistencies and they use these to pour cold water on the credibility of the plan. A common blunder is for the sales forecast to be inconsistent with the predicted market share in a given year.

P&L statement

Each of the three financial documents has a different aim. The P&L statement compares your cost of sales with the revenue generated from sales and comes up with a net (profit) figure. A forecast P&L is based on assumptions you make concerning the cost of customer acquisition, versus the value of your share of that market. It is impossible to say in general terms what these assumptions should be; the point is that you should be clear about what your assumptions are, and state why you believe they are reasonable.

So, for example, state that you are targeting 100,000 customers in year one and 500,000 customers in year two, from which you expect to gain revenue of Y. Given customer acquisition costs of £10 per customer, you calculate your gross revenue at Z. These figures are a challenge to produce, but your VCs will be looking at them in detail and asking whether they are reasonable. This means that your assumptions must be based on the quality of your offer – e.g. if you expect to compete strongly on price, then you can expect to gain significant market share.

The chart below shows how a final revenue figure is generated in general pictorial terms.

Generating revenue assumptions

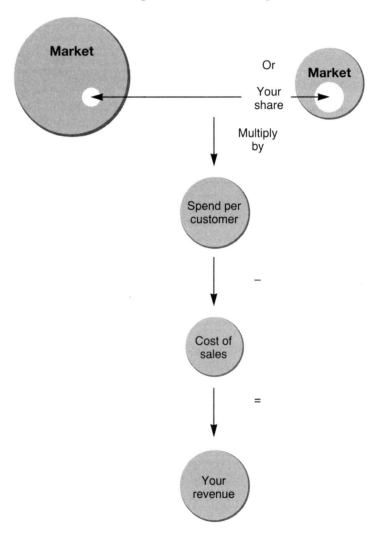

This chart also shows that your business proposition could be to take a large share of a smallish market or a tiny share of a huge market, or indeed anywhere in between. However, it is likely that your business will be directed towards an as yet untapped market, so that you can establish a substantial first-mover advantage. As one e-business adviser said: 'If your plan is to gain market share from a well-established web player, such as Yahoo!, then first phone up your doctor and ask for the men in white coats to be sent round, and then forecast your market share at 0.00001%.'

Customer acquisition costs will vary greatly from one business to the next. They usually require huge marketing spends to be successful, but B2B ideas generally rely on far smaller customer bases and therefore marketing costs are much lower.

Balance sheet

The balance sheet shows the equity and debt components of your capital and balances these against your assets, minus your current liabilities. You need to forecast simple balance sheets for about five years to show the growth of the business. This is probably the point in your plan where you will have to show when you will need extra funds from outside sources, and how much you will need to keep your assets and liabilities in balance. VCs will also assess whether your forecasts make adequate provision for working capital.

Cash flow forecast

Your cash flow forecast shows where you expect money to be coming in from and where and when it is to be going out. Most businesses have to pay for many of their inputs, such as office furniture and equipment, before they are paid for their outputs, their products and their services. The time lag effect of VAT payments (see Legals, chapter 5) is also relevant here.

There are many sites on the internet on which you can find sample business plans, so there is no need to document one here. The best site we have found at the time of writing for sample financial forecasts is pwcmoneytree.com.

Funding required

As well as appearing in the financial forecasts, the amount of money you are requesting should be made explicit in a short section of its own. This section should also explain any further action which is required from the funder, such as finding people with particular business experience not covered by those already on your team. Ideally, you should also show what the VC's exit route is, i.e. you need to state when you would expect the VC to get his or her money back. The options are (a) flotation on the stock market, (b) trade sale (purchase by another company), or (c) secondary buyout (purchase by another VC fund).

VCs do not expect you to set out your formal valuation of your business – that is their territory. Although you may have an idea of what your business is worth, you must be prepared to negotiate (see Funding, chapter 6).

Appendices

This is where you should put other relevant information, such as a disclaimer of liability, which prevents you being liable for any losses your company, and therefore the VC, might make. You might also use an appendix to explain any technical terms that are not easily explained in the main text. Also include a copy of your NDA, if a VC has already signed it (see Legals, chapter 5).

Checklist

This is a checklist of things your business plan must show:

★ you are entering a growth market;
★ you have a compelling proposition;
★ you and your team can implement the idea;
★ you are offering an exit route which will generate high returns for the investor.

The difference between bricks-and-mortar business plans and dot.com start-up business plans.

Bricks and mortar	★ Precision	★ Financial documents and forecasts are reasonably precise
	★ Speed	★ Investors expect you to spend months developing your future strategy and writing a precise plan to raise more funding
plans	★ Research	★ Marketing research and sales forecasts are reasonably precise
	★ Length	★ Bricks-and-mortar businesses have as a key component to them the actual bricks; this means that long-term, precise plans are needed before construction and development, so business plans can run to 100 pages

---

Dot.com	★ Precision	★ Often there are no past financial documents, and forecasts are rough estimates
plans	★ Speed	★ If you spend more than a few weeks writing a business plan, investors will wonder why you are letting the grass grow under your feet and potentially letting a competitor beat you to be first on the net
	★ Research	★ Some sites begin mostly as forums with the aim of selling something, although exactly what may not be clear until the site has attracted enough 'eyeballs', i.e. site visitors
	★ Length	★ Web pages can be changed rapidly, and e-business itself is changing rapidly; long-term planning is neither as necessary nor as possible, and business plans average ten to twenty pages

Appendix

Useful sites to consult when constructing business plans

bvca.co.uk
dcfor.com
pwcmoneytree.com
e-start.com
fastfuture.com
cbsc.org (no www)

CHAPTER 4
Research

'The last thing you want to do is to launch yourself on an unsuspecting market.'

RUPERT LEE-BROWNE, FOUNDER OF EGGSBENEFIT.COM

'The first step is to know who your end customers – and your prospective customers – are, and then to learn as much about them as possible. You may feel that there's no reasonable way to find out accurately who your customers are, particularly if you sell through indirect channels. But that's no longer true . . . With today's cost-effective outreach technologies . . . you can identify at least a reasonable subset of your customer base.'

PATRICIA SEYBOLD, AUTHOR OF *CUSTOMERS.COM*

'I had an idea and I thought about it. I kept on thinking, and I'm still thinking. My advice to every businessman is to read a lot and think a lot and work a lot. If he will think and think and keep on thinking, and follow up his thinking with work, he is certain to succeed.'

HENRY FORD

Introduction

You absolutely have to research. This is not an optional extra to make your business plan look a bit special, rather it must form an integral part of your plan and of your whole strategy. If you submit a plan without discussing your target market segment and your competitive positioning, the shredding machine will be but centimetres away. Why is this? Because, as one entrepreneur has put it, 'A product or service, no matter how great it is, is only worth something if people want it, and if you know who those people are. Then you have to know what will appeal to them about you that will make them buy from you rather than from anyone else out there.'

And, of course, if you want to raise money you have to convince potential funders that you have the answers to these questions, and that they are positive.

This means that first of all you have got to find out if what you can offer is something people want, then find out who these people are (for a B2B expecting a small customer base) or what kind of people they are (for a B2C requiring a huge customer base). Then you need to find out why current market players are not meeting this need, and finally, you have got to work out exactly how it is that *you* can fill this need.

Research: a myth

It is a common misconception that you cannot effectively research the online world, and therefore the online market for your product or service, due to a lack of sources. This is wrong. For any potential online business there is a range of sources because there is competition for any worthwhile business idea. Competition may come in the form of existing online competitors, offline competitors, similar online businesses, and, last but not at all least, the substitutes for your business (when the car came in, it replaced the horse-drawn carriage).

A good example of how this kind of research forms an integral part of your business model is a specialist new B2B business for the restaurant trade, eggsbenefit.com (a joke, of sorts, on eggs benedict). This business hopes to reduce inefficiencies in the way restaurants order their food supplies for the next day. Currently, at the end of each day restaurants place their order with different fruit and vegetable and meat and fish suppliers, usually by leaving messages on answering machines. Eggsbenefit enables the information to be centrally held so that only one message has to be posted for all suppliers, and creates a digital record of each order. This is co-founder Rupert Lee-Browne's version of how the business model was created:

> It wasn't that we began with an idea and then had to set about working out how to implement it and make money from it. It was rather that we sat down with representatives from the different elements in the supply chain and set about working out where the inefficiencies were. We spent a lot of time boiling down concepts and issues to try to discover what precisely was the service people needed, and how we could provide it leaving the existing supply relationships in place.

Purpose of research: know thy customer

Your aim is to know exactly what the market for your product/service is so that you can target potential customers effectively.

Understand the characteristics of your customer base by segmenting the market and understanding your chosen segment. This may not necessarily be obvious; for example, you may launch a site selling men's casual clothes, but targeted at their girlfriends/sisters as the actual purchasers who buy them.

Segmenting a market means separating customers into different groups that are:

★ big and rich enough to be worth addressing;
★ identifiable;
★ reachable.

Like a cake, you can segment a market in several different ways. The standard options include:

★ geography;
★ income;
★ socio-demographics;
★ purchasing behaviour;
★ price point.

There may be further segmentation options for any given business.

You should find out who influences buying decisions. For example, if you are launching a B2B for technology

---

software, you will need to know who the relevant advisers to the end companies are, and then target them. The number of people influencing a purchasing decision can be quite large. It can include not only the person deciding but also the budget holder, a specifier, a user, a gatekeeper and other people able to influence the process (consultants, for example).

Types of Research

There are three different types of research you can carry out: desk research, research on the telephone and face-to-face research. Desk research relies on secondary sources – materials written about your business area. The other two methods involve primary sources – sources in their own right, such as industry observers, potential customers, competitors and partners. Just to make things difficult, despite the terminology, you should consult secondary sources first and primary sources second, so that you actually know what to talk about before you start talking to people about it.

Secondary sources

Read as much as possible. You will probably be doing this already, as it is likely, and certainly desirable, that your business idea is based on an interest you have had for some time. Most start-ups are founded by people who have worked in the industry prior to leaving a company to set up their own business. Indeed, if you or one of your partners does not have this business-specific knowledge you face a steep learning curve to bring yourself up to speed, because many subscribe to the view touted by Sonia Lo, founder of ezoka.com: 'You must do what you know, because if you don't know your industry you will fail.'

But even if you know your industry, you need to formalise the research process in order to:

★ find information to flesh out your picture of who your customers are, the position of the market and the position of your competitors;
★ find names of actual contacts to talk to;
★ pick out topics of recent interest which you can use to talk both to industry observers you have isolated from your searches and to the most difficult contacts – competitors.

In addition to what you can glean from surfing, secondary sources include the following, which may be both on- and offline. Published secondary sources include:

★ books;
★ newspapers;
★ newspaper archives and cutting services;
★ magazines;
★ trade journals;
★ published market reports (from research companies such as Forrester, Fletcher Research, Keynote, Mintel, Euromonitor, Jupiter, Datamonitor, Media Metrix);
★ directories;
★ trade association handbooks;
★ government reports and statistics;
★ commercial databases.

Secondary sources that are not published for general

consumption but may be available through other routes include:

★ in-house journals and magazines;
★ company marketing literature;
★ brokers' reports;
★ consultants' reports.

Publishers

Usual sources to begin with because of the ease with which you can get hold of them are newspapers and newspaper archives. The *FT*'s website, ft.com, is an essential source of business news, archives and background information on sectors (the *Guardian*'s site, newsunlimited.com, also has a good, recent, free archive service).There are also many useful online sources for any business, from the search engines yahoo.uk.com, askjeeves.com and alltheweb.com to meta search engines (which search the search engines), such as copernic.com, to online market journals. These can be extremely useful, and snippets of them are easy to track down – try the excellent free clippings service focusing exclusively on e-business at nua.ie, and a good resource for general e-business research, perfect.co.uk/think/research/. You can then try the sites of the sources for the clippings: research firms such as jupiter.com, forrester.com, datamonitor.com, euromonitor.com, keynote.com and mintel.com. But beware: to see a full report from these sources you need to purchase it, and they can be expensive, running to thousands of pounds.

In addition, companies operating in your prospective business area will often produce marketing literature on market prospects (easy to get hold of, from the PR department), and in-house reports. These can be difficult to get hold of, especially, of course, if the company is a potential competitor. One tactic is to express particular interest in that particular company and request any recent reports they may have written, i.e. try flattery and ignorance – at least one of these will be truthful!

Government

Government reports and statistics can be very useful. You can often find them online at a government site (such as that of the Department of Trade and Industry at dti.gov.uk), and if not, the relevant government department or the Office of National Statistics will often be helpful in answering specific queries.

Brokers and advisers

Finally, brokers' reports and analysts' reports are regularly produced by the major merchant banks such as Goldman Sachs, Morgan Stanley Dean Witter, Morgan Grenfell, Deutsche Bank and Robert Fleming, and by the main management consultancy firms and accountants such as McKinsey, Boston Consulting Group, A. T. Kearney, Booz, Arthur D. Little, Andersen Consulting, Deloitte Touche, KPMG, PWC (Price Waterhouse Coopers) Ernst & Young, and, indeed, AMR, but the difficulty is in getting hold of them. These organisations have various regulatory reasons for not releasing them to the general public, e.g. merchant banks are prohibited from offering what could be interpreted as investment advice to individuals rather than to corporations, and indeed do not wish to be sued by a riches-to-rags individual. Furthermore, the information in brokers' reports is considered valuable to the company which spent time and money producing it, and they do not wish to pass this on at no cost to anyone other than bona fide customers. Nevertheless, most put a lot of information and the occasional report on their sites.

If you do not find anything useful on their site, still do not despair of getting hold of a report. Pretending to be a legitimate client is unlikely to be credible, but if you have any friends in any of these organisations, you may well find you can persuade them to send you the latest reports hanging around on their desks. And even if you don't, you might just be able to find a 'Third Way' by offering a relevant analyst some primary research you have done in exchange. But they are only likely to be interested if your research is good.

Whenever you use statistical sources covering market forecasts and the like, do not unthinkingly take the figures given on trust; always 'sanity check' them (i.e. apply your common sense), to check that several zeros have not been added by mistake. Furthermore, when researching market forecasts, you will generally find that different organisations produce different numbers, sometimes wildly so. The only advice is to take the mid-point of the various estimates, possibly excluding any outliers, i.e. any estimates which deviate significantly from the rest.

Limitations of secondary sources

There are two principal features of secondary sources which mean they cannot form the whole of your research. First of all, they tend to cover general-industry issues rather than those which are directly relevant to your business idea; the focus on specific businesses within a market is the vital contribution trade journals make to your research. Secondly, they are rarely completely up to date. Even if you are reading the latest stories they may be based on last year's statistics. If you are not reading the latest stories, then start. Of course, internet sources are often extremely up to date (although not always), but as the internet world changes from one week to the next, this may not necessarily help.

Primary sources

There are many different kinds of primary sources from whom you should aim to get a good picture of your target market, the characteristics of your potential customers, potential logistical partners, and your potential competitive positioning. Every contribution you receive to fill out this picture may be valuable, but the input from potential customers is essential, because it's back to that question of need again. You've got to know that customers want what you are going to be producing, and would use it and pay for it.

'We get a lot of start-ups coming in here who are obsessed with the idea of getting their site up and running. But a lot of them haven't thought enough about the business principles: is there a need for this product or service, and who will the customers be?'

MARK ELLIS, REDWOOD NEW MEDIA

Customers

You need to approach potential customers with your business idea, so that you can get to the bottom of the need they have and work out how you can best meet that need. Your potential customer base will vary significantly, depending on your business idea. If you are to launch a B2B, you may well have a very small customer base. This means you can approach the companies or actual individuals who would be purchasing your product/using your service, and if the base is small you really must do this, in order not to commit the sin of launching yourself on an unsuspecting audience.

However, if your site is to be a B2C, in order to generate high revenues you will have to have a much larger customer base, because each individual transaction will probably be smaller than that for a B2B. In this case, you will need to contact a sample of customers. This is the territory of market research, but you may not be able to talk to as many people as these firms would. However, you certainly should attempt to ask views directly from a certain number of potential customers, and given that you have no guarantee their views are representative you may wish to make each interaction count for more by making it deeper – see the end of this chapter for ways to do this.

In general, however, whoever your customers are, the questions you will put to them will be largely the same, covering the following issues:

★ Who are their current suppliers?
★ Are they happy with their current suppliers? Explore both positive features and negative features.
★ How do they choose their supplier? Explore what are known as the critical success factors (CSFs), the things a supplier must get right in order to succeed.
★ What are their contract relationships with their suppliers? Is it easy to switch?
★ How much do they pay for their existing supply relationship?
★ How much would they be willing to pay for a supplier who was new to the market but who offered a better product/service?

Remember to treat your customers sensitively. Make sure you prepare well before approaching them, because first impressions count.

Industry observers

Industry observers include, in rough descending order of usefulness, banking analysts and consultants, trade journalists, trade association officials and academics. These people often follow developments in an industry closely, and are familiar with many of the major players. They can provide a good introductory briefing to an industry or an issue within the industry, and are often helpful in putting you on to other contacts.

Each of these groups has its own agenda, of course. If you have managed to find a brokers' or consultants' report, the people named as having written it are usually game for a chat, particularly if you start by dealing with a specific point raised by the report. So, if you have managed to find a report online or offline and an analyst is credited, you can phone up and ask a detailed question on the report and then try to lure him or her into the wide-ranging questions you really want answered.

Trade journalists are keen to be the first to break any new story, and it is important to be particularly circumspect with them; they are often extremely good at detecting that something more is going on than meets the eye. But they do have the advantage of often being highly talkative and willing to share their expertise of a narrowly defined business area with people who are interested.

Trade associations are mostly helpful in providing lists of further contacts. They rarely offer opinions in order not to be seen to be promoting one firm or market segment over another, and sometimes are not willing to provide information, let alone opinions, to non-members.

Academics are rarely useful sources because they are primarily interested in furthering their research, which is usually painfully out of date, and the prospect of talking to someone who is in the world of business is usually not of interest to them – except as an object of envy, of course.

Regulators

Regulatory changes in the form of amendments to self-regulation principles, UK laws and EC directives can have profound impacts on industries. Often the impact is unexpected and unforeseen, even by the lawmakers them-selves. This means that even though you are unlikely to find out about an upcoming change in the law which no one else in the industry has discovered, and even if you do neither the person who tells you it or you may appreciate the full effects of the change, you do have to try. This means contacting relevant government departments concerning current and possible future white papers, and querying the EC directorates in Brussels about likely additions to their laws and directives.

Distributors

It is vital that you talk in depth with any potential distributors of your product/service in order to find out who can best handle the work you will be putting their way, and to discover what is the best deal you can offer your customers. If your business is to be one of delivering products to retail customers, this area of back-end fulfilment is one of the hardest to get right, and is totally vital. If you fail to deliver successfully to your customers you cannot hope your business will last, let alone grow.

In dealing with potential fulfilment or logistics com-panies you need to ask pointed questions to find out whether they will handle what you intend to be demanding from them. The reason for this is that, as one entrepreneur said, 'To be honest, I couldn't believe the awful deals delivery companies were proposing: no delivery within seven days at the first negotiation, and still we can only offer customers an a.m. or p.m. window with no deliveries at the weekend. I think this is really bad service, but there doesn't seem to be much I've been able to do about it.'

Suppliers

Potential suppliers for your product/service need to be grilled in just the same way as distributors, and for the same reasons. As well as potential finished-product suppliers you will also need web site designers and web site hosters. You may decide to have a 'beauty parade' to work out who is offering the right package and price for you.

Partners

Whatever your business and your area of specialisation, you will almost certainly need to have partners. They may be in the field of marketing; many start-ups who are well immersed in their field of specialisation take on offline media partners in order to capitalise on their contacts and brand strength, or their knowledge of supply and distribution arrangements, or even their technology. You should also consider online partnerships through links or routings with other sites (see Marketing, chapter 7). Many start-ups begin by considering technological partnerships and end up waiting to bring more and more of the technological work in-house in order to have greater control and prevent the possibility of diluting equity.

Competitors

Last, but by no means least, it is vital to get a grip on who your competitors are, and their different positions in the market. This helps you assess where you might fit in. The problem is that it is essential to talk to competitors, but difficult, because you have to be circumspect: not only will you be attempting to pinch their customers, but quite possibly some of their staff too. But you may well find competitors have the most carefully researched information about the state of the market and its future prospects. They will also have searched out and studied what they deem to be the weaknesses of *their* competitors.

The first port of call for contacting competitors is to check out their website (assuming they have one, because they may be offline businesses who have not yet gone online). This is often a mine of relevant company information, plus you may find it raises questions in your mind which you can then put to the company. The best and easiest way to follow up these and other questions is by the 'mystery shopper' route. This is an old, established practice whereby a business samples a competitor's product or service from the point of view of a customer. So, David, who is considering setting up David's Deliveries, phones up the in-town supplier, Sarah's Sendables, to find out what they are charging, when they are promising delivery, etc.

It is impossible to put too much time into researching competitors. According to Simon Darling, a dot.com entrepreneur, 'you have got to know the market space you've decided to enter. You need to have people involved who have worked in it before and you need to have done a thorough analysis of the competition. One team I met last week had looks of horror on their faces as I told them about competitors in the US and other parts of Europe of which they had been blissfully unaware.'

If you don't do the research, you will not be taken seriously by venture capitalists (see Funding, chapter 6).

Targeted customer research

Even internet entrepreneurs often spend several months on their research. This process takes in all of the above and adds a final element: testing. This is to say that once you have undertaken all the above and you are on the way to starting up the business, it is wise to carry out a feasibility test such as launching a trial site.

With a trial site, you are aiming to attract only a very few customers, but they go through the entire buying process. Easyshop.com, originally purely an underwear-selling site, began this way, spending a couple of months not advertising or marketing, and selling only the low volume of orders which came to the site without this.

Flexibility

The whole point of doing research is to check the viability of the business model your plan rests on. There is no point being dogmatic. If your research shows your original idea to be flawed, then you have to modify it or change it. Many online businesses mutate significantly in the early days as they discover more about the suppliers, distribution and customers.

For example, lastorders.com, the beer web site set up by Ian Gardiner and James Oliver, was originally based on the idea of selling late-dated beer at low prices. But when they were doing their research, Gardiner and Oliver discovered that there wasn't as much of this beer around as they had expected. In addition, they realised that handling large volumes of beer themselves would be very difficult, so they changed the business model and decided to link up with a wholesaler that stocked a wide range of beers. With this new business model, lastorders has no need for working capital because it is paid by its web customers well before it has to pay the wholesaler.

Once you are happy with the results of your research you can progress on to the next stage – sorting out the legal issues.

Appendix

Offline magazines covering e-business news

Wired
Revolution
New Media Age
E-Business
internet Business

Online publications covering e-business news

tornado-insider.com

business2.com
fastcompany.com
redherring.com
thestandard.com
internetinvestoruk.com

Research companies

Forrester Research
Datamonitor
Jupiter Communications
Media Metrix
Fletcher Research – specialises in research about the internet in the UK. It was recently bought by Forrester, and the name Fletcher is likely to disappear in the middle of 2000.
Financial Times – has several good books on e-commerce: look at business-minds.com
Online Research Agency at online-agency.com

CHAPTER 5
Legals

Reproduced by the kind permission of BVCA

'We managed to set up a company and begin trading without any "help" from lawyers.'

MARK HOLMES, SPACE2.COM

'If you're a serious entrepreneur, form a limited company. Everything else is just conversation.'

ENTREPRENEUR

Forms of Ownership

When starting up a business you need to establish what legal form the enterprise will take. In theory you have three choices: you can:

★ start work immediately if you are to be a sole trader;
★ form a partnership with one or more other people;
★ form a limited company.

These have different risk, ownership and tax consequences, but if you are planning to grow a significant business you should form a limited company. Forming a limited company is not so much the Third Way for prospective dot.coms aiming big as the Only Way. It is the only possible route to raising external funding from professional organisations such as venture capitalists. This is a simple process, and you could even do it yourself. But you may choose to ask your accountant to do it for you.

In addition to determining the structure of your company, you need to ensure that your business will comply with various different areas of law, including tax, data protection and the entire legal framework for your area of business. This last issue is more difficult for net businesses than for offline businesses, partly because a net business can reach countries which may have different regulations from the country in which the business is established, and partly because the regulations and laws on internet trading are still embryonic and developing.

Limited company

You can form a limited company with minimum hassle, and the effect is to limit the liability of all investors to the amount each actually invested in the business. A company is a separate legal entity; this prevents the owners of the company – the shareholders – being personally responsible for the losses of the business. Although a company usually has more than one owner, it is possible for one individual to create and own 100 per cent of a company.

Steps to formation

The steps you have to take to set up a limited company are:

★ **Choose a company name**. This does not have to be the same as your domain name; the only requirement is that it must not have the same name as that of another company. Telephone Companies House (01222 380801) and find out if your name has been taken. If it has, you are obliged to choose another name. Ask Companies House to send you their start-up pack.

★ **Draw up your Memorandum and Articles of Association**. These state the company's name, the location of the registered office and the object of the company, which may simply be to carry on business as a general commercial company. Note that if a company begins carrying out activities not listed, its shareholders can declare it as acting outside its prescribed sphere (*'ultra vires'*) and can legally force the activities to be stopped and have the perpetrator punished. Articles of Association can be amended and re-submitted to Companies House. Write the Memorandum and Articles of Association on to the appropriate legal forms provided by legal stationers (for about £10 to 20).

★ **Complete forms 10 and 12 of the Companies House start-up pack**. Do this in the presence of a solicitor or a Justice of the Peace and return them with your Memorandum and Articles of Association, plus a £20 registration fee. An alternative is to pay an accountant or an agent to do all this for you (find an agent under the company formation section of your local *Yellow Pages*) for around £120. Wait for five working days, and you will have your very own limited company.

Or rather its name will be owned by you. When it becomes a functioning company, you will become one of its owners in your capacity as a shareholder, and in your capacity as management you will also become a steward of the funds of other shareholders. Who these will be and how much they will own will depend on negotiations with backers (such as colleagues) and external funders (such as VCs).

Your company must have a minimum of a director and a company secretary, who can also be a director. Anyone can take on either role, provided they are not disqualified on certain particular counts, such as being underage or an undischarged bankrupt.

If you form a limited company before approaching external funders such as VCs (and it is certainly a good idea to do so) you will need to sort out the following issues regarding your present company form based on its present financial backing:

★ The name of the business, which will involve registering your domain name (and it must be a top-level one; see Technology, chapter 9), which you can do at one of the domain names registry sites. Register.com probably represents the best value for money, at £40 a name. Your name should, if possible, be short and/or descriptive of your business. Of course you will find that all the good names are taken (and some not-so-good ones too, such as the *Evening Standard*'s new online recruitment service bigbluedog.co.uk) but there are two possible ways around this. The first is that as of December 1999 domain names can be up to 67 characters long (including the ending) rather than the previous 23 characters. The second is that you can pre-register at idr.co.uk for the new Europe-wide top-level domain (TLD) name .eu. To buy pre-registered names, you can try domaindictionary.com, nic.uk, greatdomainnames.com and internic.net.

★ The total number of shares the company can sell or issue.
★ The number of shares each of the owners will buy.
★ The amount of money or other property each owner will contribute to buy their shares.
★ Who will manage the company. In general, a company's chairman and board of directors oversee the broad running and direction of the company, while the chief executive is responsible for its day-to-day running.

Equity Splits

Your answers to these questions will clearly change dramatically when you (and anyone else forming the business with you) give up your day job and commit capital to the enterprise. At this stage you will need to work out how much of the company shares (if any) are to be transferred to each employee. This will depend on the capital they are committing and the stage at which they joined the company.

As with negotiations prior to establishing a partnership, this issue is likely to be a difficult one to resolve. The usual method is to formulate a 'fair value' model by taking into account the capital contributed, and a 'risk value' model which takes into account the different times at which different people became involved.

However you resolve this issue, you should probably keep back some equity for distribution to future staff. And you must remember that as you raise external funding, your share of the equity pot will decrease. This is to say that a VC's contribution (which could easily be several million pounds) will cause the issuing of a certain, agreed-upon number of new shares. It will be a matter for negotiation what percentage of the total amount of funding capitalising the business you, your fellow founders and your staff own, and what percentage the VC owns.

Keeping records

The company is a legal entity separate from its owners; therefore, it will need a separate bank account and separate records. The money and property the shareholders pay to buy their shares, and the assets and money earned by the company, are owned by the company and not by the shareholders.

Company accounts relating to the revenue and expenses of the company must be kept and filed with the Inland Revenue. These are entirely separate from individuals' personal tax accounts. The company must report all income it has received from its business and may deduct certain expenses it has paid in conducting its business before paying corporate tax on the rest (see appendix for rates).

Finally, an annual return must be filed each year in Companies House before the anniversary of the company's incorporation (or within 28 days after that date), together with a payment of (currently) £15.

The Board's Duties

The shareholders of the company elect, at least once a year, a group of individuals to act as the board of directors, whose members are responsible for overseeing the strategic direction of the company and its major decisions. Usually, the board must be elected by enough of the owners to represent a simple majority of the outstanding shares, although a requirement of a higher vote can be made. Thus, those who hold a majority of the shares have ultimate control over the company.

Terms of employment for board directors are often for more than one year and are staggered to provide continuity. Shareholders can elect themselves to be on the board of directors. A classic case of this is a venture capitalist firm putting one of its executives, or a nominated representative, on the board.

A board of directors is legally obliged to meet at least once a year. In practice, boards generally meet around several times a year, and frequent meetings can be expected with a start-up, particularly an internet start-up.

Each director on the board is given one vote; usually the vote of a majority of the directors is sufficient to approve a decision of the board. Directors may be paid for their services, and with a start-up this may be in the form of a salary and/or equity, but payment is not obligatory. The board of directors elects the officers, i.e. managers, of the company. In an internet start-up these usually comprise chief executive, technology officer, sales and marketing officer, and often an operations officer.

Shareholders' benefits

Employees of a company who are also shareholders can, in theory, be paid in two ways, firstly with a salary and secondly by the distribution of share dividends. However, dividends are usually distributed only when profits are made, and many start-ups will be expecting to make losses for several months, or even years. What you will be generating (hopefully) are increasingly high valuations, as funders put more money into your business in progressive 'rounds' of financing. The idea, of course, is that at some stage you sell your shares and then buy that LA mansion.

Shareholders' liabilities

The company, as a separate legal entity, does not cease to exist if one or more of its owners dies. Its corporate existence lasts as long as its shareholders decide it should. A company's 'life' is usually perpetual, or ends with sale or deliberate termination.

	Sole proprietor-ship	Partnership	Limited company
Difficulty and cost to form	Negligible	Low to moderate	Low to moderate
Difficulty and cost to maintain	Low	Low	Moderate
Owner liability	High	High	Low
Difficulty of preparing tax documentation	Low	Moderate	High
Flexibility of ownership; abilit to bring in new owners	None	Moderate	High
Cost of terminating the business	Low	High	High

Taxes

It may not be what you imagined when you started up your own business, but entrepreneurs do have to deal with tax. There are three main kinds of tax you will have to worry about: Corporation tax, VAT and National Insurance.

'In this world nothing is certain but death and taxes.'

BENJAMIN FRANKLIN

Corporation tax

In the early years, corporation tax ought not to trouble a start-up too much because your business will be making losses. But you do need to tell the Inland Revenue you have incorporated your business (telling them your company name, address and directors). Despite what many entrepreneurs expect, even a lossmaking company is still obliged to submit a tax return for every accounting period. The Inland Revenue could fine you if you fail to do so.

There are other reasons why you have to think about tax even if you are making losses. If you want to take advantage of capital allowances (40% in the first year and 25% a year subsequently) on your expensive computer equipment and other assets, you have to submit a tax return. You can carry forward these capital allowances and any losses in the business to offset against future profits. But if you do not submit the tax returns, you will not be able to claim the allowances. Start-ups may also be able to make use of the three-year period introduced in the March 2000 budget, which allows spending on computer hardware and internet technology to be written off against tax.

For small companies (making profits of less than £1.5m) corporation tax is payable nine months after the relevant year-end. For larger companies there is a complex Quarterly

Instalment Payments (QIPs) system – under which companies have to forecast their profits and then pay instalments accordingly. If the Inland Revenue believes a business has deliberately underforecast its profits, it might fine it. If you have forecast losses in a tax year but then realise halfway through that you will probably make profits (and be liable to tax), you have to inform the Inland Revenue.

If your company has paid employees – and that includes directors – you have a legal obligation to set up a PAYE scheme. PAYE is the system that the government uses to get companies to collect personal taxes on its behalf, and there are penalties for not setting up a scheme. It is worth bearing in mind that companies can also choose to distribute profits to directors as dividends rather than salary. Dividends attract lower rates of tax than salary; and there is also no National Insurance to pay.

VAT

VAT – value added tax – adds 17.5% (in the UK) to the cost of items and is chargeable on most goods and services except for food, postage stamps, newspapers, books, children's clothes and train travel, among others. It is payable quarterly, accompanied by forms you send to your VAT office, which is assigned to you when you register.

VAT is collected by Her Majesty's Customs and Excise. These people have the most wide-ranging powers of investigation of almost any governmental body in the UK (more than the police, for instance), so do not mess with them! They are helpful in discussing your VAT issues with you, but turn nasty if they suspect you have been seeking to avoid paying VAT.

Almost every business is required to register for VAT once its sales cross a certain quarterly threshold. In any event, it is usually in your interest to register for VAT because as a business you are eligible to claim back the VAT you pay on goods and services your business buys.

VAT and cash flow

The way the process works is that you pay VAT on your business inputs – desks, computers, mined coal, etc. – just as if you were a consumer and had bought them in a shop. Then, if you are a business and VAT-registered, you can reclaim the VAT paid on those items or services bought for your business.

The result is a net transaction for you, except that because of the time delay between your paying VAT on an item or service and claiming that money back from the government, VAT on inputs acts as a loan from you to the government.

Likewise, you are required to charge VAT on your business outputs, i.e. what you sell, and then you pass the money you receive on to your VAT office quarterly. Because of the delay between your charging VAT on your outputs and you returning that amount to the government, VAT on outputs effectively acts as a loan from the government to your business.

Bad news for dot.commers

Profitable businesses (i.e. ones whose sales are higher than their costs) are net beneficiaries from these loans (setting aside the cost of administering the process, i.e. acting as the government's unpaid tax collector). But most net businesses do not expect to make profits for several months or years. This means that for this period of time the net effect is that the business effectively lends money to the government. So much for the government's commitment to e-business!

Another peculiarity for internet businesses is that VAT is not currently charged on services sold over the net, meaning that VAT operates only as a loan from you to the government, and not from the government to you. This situation may well change as the EU pressures member governments to speed up initiatives to apply VAT to online trading. This is quite an exercise, because the EU wants member state governments to agree to the same VAT rate for all.

National Insurance

Entrepreneurs often forget about National Insurance when drawing up their business plans; it currently adds about 12% to the employer's salary bill. Chris Sheffield, founder of Eunite, admitted that he underestimated his salary bill forgetting about National Insurance: 'It's a lot more than I expected. You don't think about these things when you're working for someone else.'

The only instance when a company is not responsible for paying National Insurance is when the employee is a freelance consultant who is paying his own tax and National Insurance, although this situation is becoming less common, as the Inland Revenue is making it harder for people to work freelance, and forcing people to change consulting contracts into employment contracts. If you have IT consultants working for you, you will no doubt hear dark mutterings from them about a new piece of tax legislation known as 'IR35'. This prevents consultants and others from working as independent contractors, and forces them to become employees, whether they want to or not.

A further National Insurance charge can hit a start-up because of the way the government taxes share option schemes. Inland Revenue-approved schemes avoid income tax and National Insurance (assuming options are held for three years), but many start-ups choose unapproved schemes and these companies, once floated, find they have to budget for substantial National Insurance bills based on the difference between the exercise of an option and the company's share price. (For a fuller discussion of share options, see People, chapter 10.)

Complying with the law

As an online business you are subject to pretty much the same laws as offline businesses. For instance, it is as much an offence to libel someone online as it is offline. But you also need to ensure you comply with online law as it has developed so far.

Offline law

You need to research the law for offline companies for your field in your country to make sure your business is falling in line with it. So, for example, if you are deemed to be providing advice, you then owe a duty of care to those who receive it. If your site's main business is not to provide advice, but it may at times contribute in a way that could be construed as doing so, you should ensure your site includes a disclaimer which states that opinions of contributors are theirs alone.

In addition to ensuring you do not breach your country's laws for offline trading, you need to consider that people can reach your site from any country, and countries' laws differ greatly. You may need to research whether your product or service breaches laws in other countries of the world. If it does, you should attach a notice to your site stating that your product/service is not intended for certain countries.

It is currently essential that you do this for EU member states because a proposed directive (of July 1999) would make it illegal to offer products in another member state without such a notice. In general, you must keep an eye on, or instruct your lawyers to watch out for, upcoming rulings from the EU.

Terms and conditions are vital

A number of law firms have built a lucrative business out of formulating web site terms and conditions. This is a vital process, and if you don't do it well yourself you should certainly employ a lawyer to do it for you.

The case of Argos provides a classic example of why this area is important. Argos's attempt to join the online revolution led to it mistakenly charging a mere £3 for a television. As thousands of customers clicked on the purchase button (one did so thousands of times) and Argos realised its mistake, so it managed to change its web site and get round to the business of telling customers that the price had been a mistake and Argos would not honour it. Some of the customers then threatened legal action if their TV was not delivered forthwith, and the case began to escalate, much to Argos's embarrassment. If the offer had been explicitly subject to a number of conditions (to confirmation of the price by the seller, and cancellation in the event of a mistake) Argos would have been in the clear.

Metatag ambush marketing

'Metatags' are words in the HTML code of a web site which search engines look at when compiling their list of sites relevant to someone's search. Your metatags should be words that are directly relevant to your site.

Some sites have attempted to attract traffic by putting popular words (often 'sex') in their metatags. This is not actually unlawful, just rather silly – if you are searching for pornographic pictures of donkeys you are unlikely to be interested in a local community plumbers' co-operative site.

Ambush metatag marketing, on the other hand, is when you put your competitors' names, logos or marketing catchphrases in your metatags in the hope of procuring some of their business enquiries. At the time of writing, there have been no rulings on this in the UK or EU, but there have been test cases in the US, and the companies who were offended against won. This implies that if companies use the practice here and cases are brought, the offending companies are likely to lose, and losing court cases is never cheap – or good PR.

How to make your site data protection compliant

One area of compliance which is important to many web businesses is data protection. You must ensure that you keep data on individuals (such as customers) in a way that complies with the Data Protection Act of 1986 and the new Act of 2000. In addition, you may need to register with the Data Protection Agency, depending on the activities of your business. The agency can be contacted on 01625 545700, and its advisers are very helpful, although you will usually have to wait a few minutes to get through to them.

The main principles of the Data Protection Act are:

★ your business has to have adequate security around electronic and certain paper storage of personal information;

★ you have to inform the people whose data you are collecting why you are storing the data and who will have access to it;

★ if you are intending to use the personal information for anything other than for basic marketing, such as for providing advice, or if your business is a marketing business, then (a) you must register with the agency if you intend to trade the personal information; and (b) you are required to ask customers whether they agree or object to receiving direct marketing from you.

Registration requires a fee of £35 per year and the completion of a very weighty bundle of documents, but as Mark Holmes of space2.com told us, 'The forms are very thick and seem to be designed to be intimidating, but you really can fill them all out yourself. And the staff at the agency are very good and will talk you through the process and the forms.'

NDAs

A non-disclosure agreement (NDA) is a document designed to safeguard the intellectual property residing in the good idea for an internet business. It is intended to prevent a VC or an adviser using your idea to start a business themselves without your permission.

Stories of would-be internet entrepreneurs being over-sensitive about the confidentiality of their idea are legion. Some people would have their grandmother sign a confidentiality agreement before telling her of their plans. While there are circumstances in which you should introduce an NDA (see below), it is not always a good idea to be too legalistic before you have an initial discussion about your idea with a venture capitalist. Many VCs refuse to sign NDAs at an early stage because of:

★ **Time**. They are so swamped with dot.com business plan proposals that they do not have the time or the legal resources.
★ **Professional pride**. They see NDAs as evidence of both arrogance on the part of entrepreneurs (in assuming their idea is unique) and a slur on the professionalism of the VC.
★ **Conflicts of interest**. They worry that signing an NDA with one company at an early stage might prevent them from investing in another company.
★ **Importance of implementation**. Many VCs now believe that the ability of the entrepreneur's team to implement an idea is more important than the idea itself.

In fact, an NDA may be unnecessary in some kinds of businesses. If you have a service business that is heavily reliant on human skills, and if you are close enough to launching to be talking to VCs, it might be almost impossible for someone to copy the idea and then beat you to market.

When to use an NDA

While it may be inappropriate to resort to an NDA when discussing a three-page summary of the business idea with a VC, some entrepreneurs argue that it is sensible to move to an NDA if a full plan is submitted because of the potential danger of someone beating you to the launch if word gets round about the idea. Some product-based business ideas might be particularly at risk. Some observers cite a case in the US where kozmo.com alleged that venture capitalists had used information it had provided to set up a competitor, urbanfetch.com. Urbanfetch claimed that no confidentiality agreement had been signed.

According to Steven McDonald of grifkin.com, signing an NDA is common sense:

> It's a bit like asking an employee not to sign an employment contract and saying, 'Oh, we'll look after you.' The thing is, you can never be sure. And while there are people (very few, I might add) doing unpleasant things to each other, it is best to demand that you need to protect your interests. The other benefit is that upon signing the NDAs, we find that openness begins to flow in both directions, which makes for much more productive communication.

Entrepreneurs without an existing relationship with a VC might want to take some other precautions:

★ only submit a three-page summary in the first instance rather than a full plan;

★ check a VC's web site to see if there are any similar investments that might present a conflict of interest;

★ ask at the start of a meeting with a VC whether there are any undisclosed investments in the same area as your business;

★ avoid leaving material or extensive research with the VC at an early stage (as Promod Haque of Norwest Venture partners said: 'Don't spill your guts.').

You will certainly need an NDA if you discuss your plan with any potential partners, particularly if they are larger companies. Although these companies might be friendly now, they could still become powerful competitors in the future. The risk of giving away vital commercial knowledge to potential partners is much larger than when talking to VCs.

A sample NDA is available from VentureDirectory's web site, at venturydirectory.com/nondisclosagr.htm, or from Ross & Co at its web site, eTradeLaw.com.

Confidentiality agreements

However, in the later stages you will certainly need a confidentiality agreement, which will be signed by potential funders and their advisers. A confidentiality agreement aims to secure agreement with the party gaining access to the information that this information

★   is secret;
★   is only to be used for the purposes for which it is being made available;
★   will not be disclosed to any other party without express written permission from you;
★   will be returned to you when no longer needed.

The agreement may also contain a provision for damages if it is breached.

A sample confidentiality letter is available from the British Venture Capital Association at bvca.co.uk, or telephone 0207 240 3849.

Intellectual Property

Because of the novelty of the internet, the legal framework is still undergoing rapid development. However lawyers working with dotcom companies say intellectual property is a potential minefield for internet start-ups. The three major areas are:

★ **Patents.** Although you cannot patent an idea, patent law does potentially allow internet companies to entrench first mover advantage. For example, US law currently allows companies to patent business models – and this allows companies like Amazon to try to protect its one-click ordering system and Priceline its reverse auction process (where buyers say what they are prepared to pay). European patent law is currently less permission than that in the US but it still allows companies to protect certain groups of ideas (as in offline publishing) and it would well follow the US lead as it develops – as it has done in the cast of software.

   If you write your own software, you may (unwittingly) infringe another company's patented software – especially if your website is available in the US (and most are). If you licence software, you must make sure that you are indemnified against being sued by another software company for breach of patent.

★ **Copyright.** Because it is easy to download material from a website, you have to consider whether you need to protect what you show. If you own the copyright of the material yourself, you may need to consider protecting any valuable images with logos or other devices. Many sites also show material (visual or aural) where the copyright is owned by a third party. You need to warn viewers that these materials are protected by copyright – otherwise you could be held to be assisting duplication.

You also need to make sure that your software and web designers assign the copyrights of software and web page design to you. Otherwise there is a possibility that they could try to prevent you moving to other suppliers for updates.

★ **Trademarks.** When you register your domain name, you should be careful that you do not choose the same name as an established trademark. This might appear to be an easy task (i.e. don't pick Harrods). But the international nature of the web means that if you are planning future expansion, you must also make sure that your domain name does not potentially infringe the trademark of a company in another country that you may not have heard of. You also need to consider registering your domain name as a trademark to prevent someone else from doing so.

Because the internet is relatively new many of these potential problems have yet to come to the surface in the UK – let alone to court. But several acrimonious law suits have already taken place in the US, and lawyers think that it is only a matter of time before these cases start to crop up in the UK. According to Lyn Barcow of Withers, if you make mistakes over intellectual property 'you either have to defend yourself or to give way. Either way it is very expensive – especially if foreign courts are involved'.

Hiring lawyers

> Q: 'What do you call two hundred lawyers
> at the bottom of the ocean?'
> A: 'A good start'

As we have seen, you can do a lot of the initial paperwork involved in setting up a company yourself without any aid from lawyers, provided you are prepared to tackle the nitty-gritty and approach matters with a critical eye. However, sooner or later you will need the services of lawyers. You will need to choose a firm to act for you, and to agree the appropriate (i.e. lowest) staff level. But how do you choose a firm of lawyers?

There are online services from the established law firms, such as cliffordchance.com and linklaters.com, and others can be expected soon. These are aimed at large corporations, not start-ups, unless they are very well funded. However, there are several good law firms who specialise in internet law, including Bird and Bird (twobirds.co.uk), Hobson, Audley and Wood (hobsonaudley.com) and Rakisons (rakisons.co.uk). An alternative is the Law Society's 'lawyers for your business' scheme, whereby local lawyers will offer you an initial consultation free of charge. The Law Society are on 020 7405 9075.

The best thing to do when looking to establish a relationship with a firm of lawyers is the same as with any other service provider, including management consultants and plumbers: ask your friends and contacts who they have used. Approach a few alternative suppliers, and see who you get on best with. If the first firm doesn't provide what you want, then change.

How lawyers charge

★ **Flat fees**. There are certain standard costs for certain standard activities, such as witnessing certain documents.

★ **Hourly fees**. Although frighteningly expensive, an hour for a senior lawyer (up to £350) can be a better deal than longer with a less experienced lawyer. Whenever hourly fees are to be charged, it is always sensible to place a cap on the fee, with an agreement to discuss a future course of action should the lawyer say more work is necessary.

★ **Contingency fees**. This is where the lawyer's fee is dependent upon a positive outcome. This is an inappropriate charging structure for most issues other than litigation, which is legalese for non-criminal disputes.

★ **Additional expenses**. These will be charged for travel, long-distance phone calls, etc. Some additional expenses you might not expect are also chargeable to you, e.g. photocopies of a document to be given to opponents and barristers, although copies for the lawyer's internal purposes should not be charged to you. Likewise, overnight deliveries will be charged to you when they are in response to emergencies, but not when they arise as a result of the slowness of the lawyer.

★ **Equity**. Lawyers (like other advisers) are increasingly accepting fees in equity, or equity options, i.e. fees they hope to realise and collect upon at some later, often unspecified, date. This minimises the amount you need to cough up early on, but also further dilutes your equity stake, which you may wish to avoid.

Always demand a fully broken-down bill!

Appendix

Personal income tax rates (2000–2001)

Up to £4,385	0%
next £1,500	10%
next £1,501–£28,000	22%
Over £28,000	40%

Corporate tax rates (financial year to 31.3.2000)

Full rate	30% (i.e. for profits over £300,000)
Small companies rate	20% (i.e. for profits below £300,000)

VAT

Standard rate	17.5%
Registration level	£51,000 p.a.

Online law references

lectlaw.com
vcr1978.com
theogoddard.com
The Law Society (020 7405 9075)

Specialist internet lawyers

Bird and Bird (twobirds.co.uk)
Hobson, Audley and Wood (hobsonaudley.com)
Rakisons (rakisons.co.uk)

Sample legal documents can be downloaded from digitalpeople.org

CHAPTER 6
Funding

Reproduced by the kind permission of BVCA

'For VCs at the moment it is like standing in front of a hosepipe trying to drink water – you get swamped.'

PAUL VICKERY, 3i

'Some VCs think they add value, but don't. Some clearly say they won't add value, they just add cash. But what you really want is VCs who say they will add value, and do. So you start by looking for VCs who have done it before for a business like yours.'

MICHAEL ROSS, FOUNDER OF EASYSHOP.COM

'Your starting capital, which lets you give up the day job and start working on the idea, should come from three sources: friends, family and fools.'

HERMANN HAUSER, AMADEUS CAPITAL.

'Never surprise your VC.'

SONIA LO, FOUNDER
OF EZOKA.COM

The moneyed meet the brilliant but broke. It can be a perfect match, provided each side knows what they are getting for what they are giving up. There are many different sources of funding, and they all offer different things with different strings attached.

You should work out what level of support you need and when you will need it. If you have a plan and a whole team, including someone with management experience, then venture capital may be perfect. But if you only have an idea then you probably need to approach family and friends or business angels. If you have an idea and a plan you might try an 'incubator' – an organisation that nurses business ideas through the start-up stage. Or you might approach one of the new internet funds that straddle the boundary between venture capital and incubators.

It is just possible that you may not need significant outside funds to get your business started. There are several examples of internet start-ups that have been established with very modest resources. The-bullet.com, a site that provides a quick summary of newspaper headlines, was set up without venture capital and is now modestly profitable. HotBox, a web site for gadgets for men, was set up in a Cardiff garage with £1,000 and is now achieving sales of £5,000 a day. HotBox has recently raised some extra money for expansion. So even if you manage to start your business in the box room, you could go on to raise enough funds at some stage to get the business properly established.

Traditionally, there were four funding stages in setting up a company: seed capital, start-up, early stage and expansion. Even though these terms are still used by many of the people who provide cash, this structure is breaking down because internet companies are developing so fast. Some of the larger venture capital firms that used to concentrate on financing expansion of more established firms are now looking at start-ups or early-stage financing with new interest because the returns can be mouth-watering. Some incubators are also prepared to invest cash as well as provide services and support.

Seed capital

Your savings may not be enough to start your start-up. You may have no savings at all. The next obvious place to look for seed capital is friends and relations. Look hard. Even though you may not think it, you may have a rich relative somewhere, and even if they are not willing to help, they might put you in touch with a rich friend or contact who is. The advantage of friendly sources of cash is that you may be able to negotiate less onerous terms than with commercial sources, although people are increasingly aware of the potential value of new business ideas and of course they will usually expect equity in return for their cash.

Another source of seed capital is business angels. These are private individuals who invest money in the form of equity in entrepreneurial businesses that require finance for growth at an early stage in their development. A business angel typically invests between £10,000 and £200,000. Some angels want to invest in the same sector where they made their own money, and want to be involved in running the business; others are simply looking for promising invest-ments.

How to find an angel

The challenge for any start-up is to find a suitable angel and to find one that wants to invest. The British Venture Capital Association (bvca.co.uk) publishes a directory of angels that includes details of regional angel groups called EquityLinks. The National Business Angels Network (NBAN) (nationalbusinessangels.co.uk), formerly known as LINC, has almost 500 investors on its books, and there are regional associations as well. For example, in London LEntA Ventures has access to about 75 investors and operates a matching service for promising companies. NBAN charges £100 for a company wanting to register and it also offers the services of associates (at a charge) to help companies present to investors more effectively.

There are many useful sites which link entrepeneurs to angels, such as angelmoney.com, garage.com and vcr1978.com. Generally you need to submit brief business plans for assessment.

Business archangels

Richer than angels, easier to locate, but harder to contact, are business archangels. These are individuals with huge resources who may choose to back a start-up if they like the technology or some other aspect of an entrepreneur's proposal. Archangels include Paul Allen (co-founder of Microsoft), Ben Rosen (chairman of Compaq), Sandy Robertson (founder of Robertson Stephens), David Potter of Psion and Bernard Arnault (chairman of LVMH). If you do manage to catch the interest of an archangel they can provide contacts and expertise as well as funding.

However well-heeled, business angels and archangels

are not altruists and they look for serious returns on their investments, although they may not be as thorough and painstaking as venture capitalists when assessing proposals from start-ups. An angel may be able to make a decision much more quickly, especially if the start-up is in a sector that he or she knows.

Angels and syndicates of angels are unlikely to want to take a majority stake in a start-up and are unlikely to invest huge sums. If large sums are needed, an entrepreneur usually has to approach venture capital companies.

Finding Venture Capital

What are venture capital and private equity?

There is some confusion about the terms 'private equity' and 'venture capital'. Private equity refers to funds provided to unquoted companies both large and small. Strictly speaking, venture capital is a subset of private equity and refers to investments in start-ups or early stage businesses. In Europe however the terms are often interchangeable. The money for venture capital investments usually comes from institutions, or from internal funds.

Venture capitalists provide equity capital for up to around five years for businesses starting up or in the early stages of growth. They take a share in the business, which is to say they provide cash in return for an equity stake. They do not seek day-to-day management control of the company, although they usually want to appoint a director to the board (or take this function themselves) to share their considerable experience in start-ups, and also to safeguard their interests. The average size of venture capital investment in 1999 was £3.4 million, but this masks a wide range of investments, from £100,000 to £50 million.

Equity capital does not give the VCs a guaranteed return; rather, their return is dependent upon the growth and profitability of the business. This is good for you because it means their incentive is the same as yours: the success of the business. VCs are not Gordon Gekkos with an interest in company wrecking, they enable companies to grow and compete; they are an important source of business experience, contacts and advice, as well as just cash. According to Ferdinand Porak, a venture capitalist at Dresdner Kleinwort Benson, 'I expect to monitor very closely a company I invest in. This is the key to success. If they are just looking for money, I am not interested. I expect to help. I would therefore normally seek a board seat. Only then can I really add value with financial and investment banking expertise. I can also help with contacts, technical support and market information.'

'When we started, we didn't think we needed venture capital; we thought that between us we had the skills to do it.'

JOSEPHINE MUNROE, CO-FOUNDER OF THE-BULLET.COM.

What to do first

The first port of call for anyone seeking venture capital or private equity is the British Venture Capital Association. It has a very useful web site (bvca.co.uk) which lists its 126 full and 123 associate members. Associates are advisers, including lawyers, accountants and management consultancies such as AMR. It is vital to research funders because you need to know which ones deal with your business area, stage of business and amount you need.

3i is the largest provider of venture capital in Europe. Paul Vickery explained how 3i assesses internet start-up business plans:

★   We are only interested in pan-European concepts. This is because anything in the UK is facing competition from the US, and given that 90% of internet business ideas are copies from the US, it's only a matter of time before most of them face serious competition from their big brothers across the water. So it is vital to create barriers to entry, and having a pan-European business is one such barrier.

★   Then our interest will depend upon the sector chosen. For example, if the sector is books or CDs then we say forget it, because that sector is covered. Also some other sectors are very difficult to enter, such as DIY or gardening services, because these depend heavily upon a strong logistical effort. This is difficult because the infrastructure to implement them is not readily available here yet, i.e. you cannot buy off-the-shelf a managed warehouse, a system to track delivery, or an efficient way of delivering the product. Instead you need to hire these separate elements, and this is expensive.

★   Then we look at the management team. We are looking for a mix of creative spark, which is difficult to convey in a business plan, and good business experience. We need to see how the team intends to execute the business plan through their network of contacts. This means that those without good CVs do not get far. If a good team was not in place, the idea would have to be exceptional, and then we would find a CEO.

Private equity groups are involved with many other areas apart from start-up companies, so it is important to make a careful selection of potential firms. Different venture capitalists look at different sectors and have different selection criteria. You should find out as much as you can about a firm before approaching it in order to increase your chances of success. Venture capital firms are in close contact with each other, and if you approach a VC with a promising idea they will often organise a funding syndicate.

There are new venture capital firms springing up all the time, and the information held by the BVCA may not always be comprehensive. In addition, American venture capitalists are taking an increased interest in the opportunities in the UK and Europe, and US institutional investors are pouring money into venture capital. According to a survey by Price Waterhouse Coopers, investments of venture capital in US entrepreneurial ventures rose from $14.2 billion in 1998 to $35.6 billion in 1999, with the bulk going to technology-based companies. More money was invested in the last quarter of 1999 than in the whole of any previous year. The NVCA (the US version of the BVCA) has information on US venture capitalists, such as General Atlantic, who are investing in Europe.

What criteria do you need to meet to be able to raise VC money?

Before approaching VCs, you must be prepared to:

★ give up equity in the company in exchange for money;
★ agree a valuation of your business (see below);
★ share your business idea: would-be entrepreneurs often approach VCs and chatter excitedly about how they have an amazingly brilliant idea, and then refuse to say what it is; see Legals (chapter 5) for a discussion of non-disclosure agreements, or (NDAs).

What are all venture capitalists looking for?

'VCs want a sensible idea and a great business team.'

SUSAN KISH, FOUNDER OF ZURICH'S FIRST TUESDAY

Venture capitalists have various criteria for selecting possible investments but common ones include:

★ A good business idea in a promising sector.
★ A good team. Venture capitalists look very closely at the track record of the team members in order to judge whether the company will have the ability and deter-mination to implement the idea. They may also look for both online and offline experience in the targeted industry sector.
★ A company at the right stage. Do you have the idea and the core team, are you ready to go? If not, you may need an incubator instead (see below).
★ An aggressive growth plan. VCs are not interested in a business which is going to pootle along; you've got to be aiming big and fast. Why? Because the VCs are taking a significantly greater risk than standard equity invest-ment, and will only do so on the expectation of a significantly greater return. This means that you probably have to be forecasting returns of around 30% to 40% compound per annum.
★ Research into market and competitors.
★ Understanding of market position and USP.
★ A good match with the VCs' preferred area of investment.
★ International potential. Many VCs are not interested in

'You can't go to a VC if you haven't got a chief technology officer on board because they won't believe you can jump the hurdles.'

CHRIS FROST,
FOUNDER OF
ONSENIORS

ventures which are restricted to just one country.

★ A plausible exit route. The VCs usually need to get their money back out within a few years (see below).

Some venture capitalists try to be ahead of the entrepreneurs by researching promising sectors themselves. According to Paul Vickery of 3i, 'We do research and focus on gaps that are available in the market. We're not waiting for business plans to come to us. For example, there is a huge market for healthcare and we are going out talking to US players to see what they are doing and what their plans are here, so that we can benchmark the approach by management teams here.'

What do you show them?

Your first approach should probably be an executive summary (see Plan, chapter 3). Boil your idea down to two or three pages, something that will grab the attention but not take up much time. Some venture capitalists insist on a maximum of three pages for the initial screening process.

Venture capitalists certainly won't devote much time to your proposal unless they are immediately attracted to the idea. Your aim in sending the summary is to secure a meeting. Don't expect any more than this. And, as with all aspects of entrepreneurship, persistence is everything: if you don't hear an answer, pester.

It's also important to select carefully which venture capitalists to approach. If a VC's interests match your requirements, try and check which other companies have been taken on. You need to show why you are approaching a particular venture capitalist; the application must not appear like a mail-out.

It is useful to include a letter of recommendation about your proposal from anyone you think may sway the mind of the venture capitalist reviewing your proposal. An endorsement from someone involved in a net business, someone who has raised money from venture capitalists in the past, or even a dot.hon (a famous or well-connected person – either a member of the 'digerati', or a big cheese from the offline world) might make all the difference. This is where schmoozing and networking can pay dividends.

According to Simon Havers, a director of ABN Amro Private Equity, you have to check that your proposal falls within the VC's criteria for investment before trying to show that you can offer a sufficient return:

> There is no point in force-feeding them your pitch in the hope of impressing them so much that they alter their criteria for you, because they won't. Your time would be better spent pitching to your local shop assistant in the hope that she'd just inherited a fortune.
>
> Your opening sentence should be, 'I am looking to raise £X million now and a further £Y million in the next 12 months, and in the last 12 months the total revenues of my company were £Z million (even if Z is nil). Is your fund open-minded to investing in such companies?' The majority of private equity providers will say no at this point, in which case you should just say goodbye and go find something better to do with your time.

How long does the whole process take?

A typical investment process from the start, when the VC receives and reviews the business plan, to the finish, when the VC actually invests in the company, traditionally takes between three and six months. But internet start-ups are much faster, and the process can take as little as six weeks, although the due diligence process (see below) may extend this.

The process begins with the initial contact with the VC and proceeds to an 'offer letter', which sets out the general terms of their proposal to you, although it is not binding on any party. The offer letter demonstrates the investor's commitment to your team's business plan and shows that serious consideration is being given to making an investment.

Then, provided that research into the business and the market by the VC and their agents is satisfactory, a new company is normally set up to acquire the relevant assets of the start-up and receive the cash of the VC. The use of a new company minimises the risk (to the VC) of liability to unknown law suits.

Due Diligence

'Despite what you hear about a wall of money, the reality is that VCs are not throwing money around, they're selective.'

RICHARD DOWNS, CO-FOUNDER OF IGLU.COM

Even if a venture capital firm is enthusiastic about a proposal, it will probably spend time checking the details of the plan. There would be basic checks, for instance, on the claims in the business plan about the markets and customers. A VC might commission research on the technology if that was a key part of the proposal. There would probably be financial and legal due diligence too. On a big enough deal, the VC might also commission commercial due diligence, in which a firm of management consultants reviews the market and the competition, and comments on the robustness of the business plan.

Venture capitalists also try to avoid dealing with fraudsters, or people who simply exaggerate. They sometimes employ private detectives to check the personal records of the team applying for money. If there are too many suspicious statements, the VC may start to question the integrity of those involved and the soundness of the business plan. The offer of funding might be withdrawn.

Some entrepreneurs find that raising finance takes far longer than they expect. 'If we were starting again,' says Maxine Benson, co-founder of everywoman.com, 'I would get funding in place before starting the business because getting funding is very time-consuming and draining. Starting a business is tough enough, but trying to raise funding and start a business at the same time is very, very tough.'

Can you seriously hope to get VC funding?

There are many sites on the web that complain at length that VC finance is very hard to raise. This may be true, but it doesn't prove that *you* will not be able to raise VC money, only that you have got to be able to be *good* to raise VC financing, and lucky. You should acknowledge the numbers game VCs face, rather than conclude that VCs have a malicious wish to reject nearly every idea they see. As the head of Edison Venture Fund says, 'We see 2,000 business plans a year, of which we might visit 300, seriously consider and conduct due diligence on 50, and invest in perhaps ten.'

While the statistics may look forbidding, there is evidence that it is becoming easier to find venture capital than in the past. UK venture capital companies are now much more willing to consider investing in start-ups than in the past. Traditionally, UK venture capital put far more money into buyouts and buy-ins of established companies than start-ups. But that is now changing. About four years ago, Neil Crofts of Razorfish took an internet business idea to some venture capitalists, 'but they did not know what I was talking about'. Now, he says VCs are putting money into internet ideas very readily.

If you have a business that is already running and you are generating revenues, you are likely to be in a much stronger bargaining position with VCs. In fact, you may well be able to choose your backers. According to Anna Russell, marketing director of silicon.com, the issue then is choosing 'the right money. It's about picking the partners who you trust and admire and who are going to help you. It's more than just money.'

There is anecdotal evidence that start-up companies are now able to drive better deals with venture capital companies (twice as much money for the same equity stake, or the same cash for half the equity stake) than a year ago simply because there is so much hot money chasing internet stocks. Of course, this bubble may burst at any time, but hopefully not before you read this book!

VCs are not the only option

If an entrepreneur fails to impress UK VCs sufficiently to raise funds, there are an increasing number of other potential sources. These include:

★ incubators;
★ corporate investors;
★ US investors;
★ AIM-quoted investment funds.

Incubators

Although well established in the US, incubators are still relatively new in the UK. An incubator helps a company that is still in embryonic form with advice, facilities and sometimes money for up to six months in return for equity. Practical help which may be available includes office space and assistance with finding appropriate personnel.

A good incubator will help you identify and achieve the various technical and practical hurdles before the business can be launched. After a period of development, an incubator may help a company raise further funds. Many incubators have close links with venture capital firms, and others with business schools and advisory firms.

If all this sounds very attractive, it is. The catch is that good incubators take on less than 1% of the business ideas submitted. They also take an equity stake in return for the services and cash. Some incubators expect a stake of 50% for their services! Because companies tend to be at an early stage of development, incubators look even more searchingly at the emerging business idea and the competitive position.

Consultant Incubators

Several incubators have been set up by management consultants. Bainlab, for example, offers financial, technical and strategic support for promising projects and has a £25 million fund for investment in start-ups. A. T. Kearney has a $1.5 billion fund, and Andersen Consulting has earmarked $1.2 billion for internet and technology start-ups. McKinsey has a 90-day 'accelerator centre' for internet start-ups. Ernst & Young favours technology start-ups rather than consumer ideas, but sometimes prefers to sell the ideas at an early stage to big companies rather than develop an independent company.

Consultants have mixed motives for being involved in internet start-ups: a promising start-up company today may become a valuable source of fee income in the future and the knowledge can be leveraged to generate huge fees from advising established companies about e-commerce. In addition, the incubators offer a way of stemming the haemorrhage of talented staff consultants to dot.coms by allowing them to develop ideas in-house.

Companies chosen by consultant incubators are often enthusiastic about the experience. Jac Peeris, a former Bain consultant and founder of skillvest.com, a corporate training web site, said: 'Getting selected is a big hurdle, but once you're selected you have access to an amazing set of resources.' Chris Sheffield, founder of eunite.com, a designer of interactive web sites and interactive digital television equipment, said that Deloitte's incubator 'gave me a sanity check. I was naïve. I thought I had a great idea and that people would want to hand over cash. But it does not happen like that. Deloitte helped me with my plan and produced much more robust sales forecasts. They also helped me to raise further funds from 3i.'

But entrepreneurs should be realistic about what incubators can provide. Some incubators will not consider internet proposals from entrepreneurs without team members already in place to cover technology. 'The market is so tight that you can forget trying to recruit someone on the technology side,' commented Ernst & Young's Alan Dawson.

Business school incubators

Incubators are also being established by leading business schools. For example the London Business School set up an incubator in 1999, available to alumni or teams involving someone who has been to the school. Cranfield business school is shortly to offer access to an incubator as part of its MBA. Students will have the chance to start an e-business as part of their course.

Boutique incubators

Below the level of the big consultants, small boutique incubators are springing up like mushrooms. These offer a much less consistent level of assistance and finance. Some offer little more than a serviced office, while others offer venture capital under a different label. You need to assess very carefully what is on offer, and the experience of the executives. Be very clear about what you are getting, especially if you are being asked to exchange equity (which you will). Try to speak to someone who has already had a business incubated there.

'You have to be very careful about incubators . . . A lot of incubators ask for half of your company.'

CHRIS FROST,
FOUNDER OF
ONSENIORS

It may be worth monitoring which companies in which sector have been supported by which investor. This information is sometimes mentioned in the *FT*, and shareholders are always mentioned in listing particulars (look for companies floating on the AIM or main stock market). Another way of tracking investors is at koldoon.com, which has a list of 6,500 companies and their funders.

Corporate investors

A number of major companies have set up funds to invest in start-ups or developing companies. Reuter's Greenhouse Fund (reuters.com/greenhouse/) is one of the best-known examples. It has invested in about 36 companies, including

Yahoo!, when its founders were still at college. Some other big companies invest together through private funds. For example, Vivendi, the French utilities group, is the largest shareholder in Viventures, a fund run from Paris and San Francisco that also includes Nokia, Cisco and Mannesmann among its shareholders. Viventures' better-known investments include QXL and chateauonline.

Company funds tend to be interested in investing in companies in or close to their own sector. Reuters particularly interested in companies that offer innovation in areas close to its core business of financial information and communications technology. Bass, a large owner of hotels, recently took a stake in lastminute.com.

A start-up company might get a very direct 'no' from a major company (although much may swing on who you approach and how you approach them). But there is evidence that many major companies are now seeing the attractions of investing in start-ups within their sector:

★ **Low cost**. What represents a significant investment in a start-up may be a modest sum for a major company.
★ **Speed**. A start-up may be able to develop an idea much faster than an in-house team, stifled by big-company bureaucracy.
★ **Low risk**. A company may be able to explore a new approach within a start-up without completely reorganising its existing business.
★ **Insurance**. An investment in a small company might represent an inexpensive option providing insurance against possible web-based changes in the sector.

The risk for the entrepreneur is that you may give away the details of the plan to a more powerful and richer rival. A big company has a completely different agenda from a venture capitalist and might decide to neuter a new competitor.

US investors

Having made huge profits on US internet business, many US institutions see Europe as the next promising internet investment opportunity. While groups such as Amadeus Venture have been operating in Europe for some time, scarcely a day goes by without another group announcing a major fund. In February 2000, Carlyle Internet Partners and Puttnam, for example, both announced $500 million European internet funds. The attraction of US funds to UK entrepreneurs is that US VCs have a much longer record of investing in start-ups.

AIM-quoted investment funds

In the second half of 1999 and the first few months of 2000 there has been a rash of companies set up on the AIM to invest in internet businesses. We have mentioned many of these companies in the appendix to this chapter, but the list of companies is growing all the time. Some of these groups are linked to boutique incubators (see above) and others seek to invest in particular aspects of the web or particular parts of the UK. Given that the purpose of many of these companies is to provide funds, they are certainly worth considering. Again, it is important to look at the track record of the funder and whether the terms of the exchange of equity for cash is reasonable.

Other funding options

★ **Internet matching services**. These web sites match entrepreneurs with venture capitalists, angels and other funds (see appendix).

★ **Intermediaries**. These can be very useful, but you have to pay for them. Brokers charge only if they achieve funding for you, but you pay agreed fees to advisers whatever the outcome.

★ **Government**. It's worth applying for government grants for small businesses, but these are only ever going to be a small amount of the total. Regional development funds may be a better bet than central government.

★ **Trusts**. A small number may be worth approaching. For example, the Prince's Trust is reported to have put £10,000 into surfworld.com, a site for surfing enthusiasts. However, the Prince's Trust is restricted to those under 30 who have already tried other sources of funds.

★ **Banks**. They do provide start-up loans for small businesses, but they're pretty small, and the penalties for reneging are substantial. Clearing banks (like Barclays) primarily provide reasonably small-scale overdrafts and short- to medium-term loans at fixed, or more usually variable, rates. The underlying problem is that bank managers are trained to look at businesses with assets (which can be used as collateral) rather than start-ups.

You and your funders

You want hard cash from funders. But the amount you can raise depends on the valuation of your company.

The valuation of internet companies is a black art. The figure the VC comes up with for what your business idea is worth – in the sense of its potential value as an operating business – may be very different from your calculation. But remember, it is not your job to be making the VC an offer based on a particular valuation of your company; and neither is it your job to value companies (unless, of course, it is!). So be prepared to walk away if the offer is much lower than you were expecting/hoping for, but also be prepared to change your opinion if you consider that you could actually get the business going with that amount of money.

There are several different ways of valuing a start-up company. These depend on making forecasts of customers, sales and profits for the business. These will be the key variables that determine its potential value:

★ **Discounted earnings multiple**. This approach looks ahead to the time when a company breaks into profit. The profits are forecast, and discounted backwards to achieve a current value. Clearly both the profit figure and the appropriate discount rate are figures that could be the subject of intense debate.

★ **Peer group performance**. This method looks at valuations placed on similar businesses to the start-up. The most obvious way is to compare the market value of a quoted company with its profits, sales, number of customers or the number of visitors to its web site. If a quoted company is not available, it may be possible to make a similar comparison with an unquoted company that has changed hands, or where a stake has changed hands for money. These ratios can then be used to value the start-up at some point in the future (assuming targets have been met). Adjustments would have to be made to take into account the competitive position of the companies: a market leader would have a higher valuation than a newcomer. Different ratios apply to different sectors, depending on the likely value of the revenue stream from a customer. For example, an online stockbroker might be worth £150,000 per customer, a community site just £150. Freeserve, often used as a comparator by hopeful entrepreneurs, floated with a value of £1,500 per customer, and is now valued at almost £5,000 per customer.

★ **Relative P/E**. It may be possible to compare the stock market value and expected future earnings of quoted companies with the start-up. But because few internet companies are making profits, this approach requires many assumptions.

★ **Leverage potential**. Because it is often difficult to find comparators for internet businesses, a valuation is sometimes based on an assessment of how much it would cost an existing business to acquire a certain number of customers or market share.

These different approaches may yield quite different results. A negotiation about valuation might consist of a discussion about which of these approaches is more appropriate. But anyone familiar with internet businesses knows how difficult it is to 'value' them. Ultimately, the venture capitalist's offer may be based as much on gut-feel as calculation.

No one ever thinks the company is worth what the valuation says it is, but it's either worth nothing or millions. So people place a bet. The real question with valuations is what the 'market price' is for companies at our stage of development, so it's whatever the going rate is. At the end of the day, we all want to do a deal and get on with it.

MICHAEL ROSS, FOUNDER OF EASYSHOP.COM

Pre- and post-money valuations

An example of how the interaction between the valuation of your company and size of the equity stake that is handed over to the VC works is as follows.

A start-up with three million fully diluted shares valued at £1 per share has a pre-money valuation of £3 million. An investor invests £1 million to buy one million newly-issued shares. The company now has a £4 million post-money valuation and four million fully diluted shares. So the investor received a 25% stake in the start-up in exchange for his £1 million investment.

'Fully diluted' means that the number of shares not only includes all outstanding shares, options and warrants, etc., but also any shares, options and warrants that are authorised, but not yet issued or granted. Options, which give their owners the guaranteed option to buy more shares at a certain price, are likely to be vital to attract high-quality staff to your company and keep them there. This means that in determining the valuation of a company you should usually create a sufficiently large option pool that can be used to attract necessary management talent and key contributors until the next round of financing.

How much money **should** you raise, and how long **will it last**?

Different businesses need different amounts of money. Seed capital might run to £250,000 for a new idea. A first round of venture capital money might raise up to £3 million with individual firms contributing up to £1.5 million each. Venture capitalists tend to be well connected and usually form a syndicate if a strong idea needs substantial backing. Each round of funding should be expected to get the business to the next 'deliverable' – the first prototype, the first customer, etc. – which is usually expected to be up to 18 months away. It is rare for a tranche of capital to be designed to last the business fewer than 12 months, partly because the discussions with venture capitalists are time-consuming and can be a distraction from management of the business.

How much equity do you have to give away?

There are no hard-and-fast rules about how much equity you will have to give away to raise a given amount of cash. It all depends on your bargaining position: how much money you need balanced by the venture capitalist's perception of the attractiveness of your business. It is not unusual for a company to give up to 25% of its equity away at each stage of financing, leaving its founder with only a minority after the second round of financing and perhaps only 15% or 20% at final flotation or trade sale. This may sound a small slice of the cake to be left with, but if the business is attractive and growing fast, the 'small stake' could be worth a fortune – literally.

There is some evidence that it is better to battle on with private money or money from one backer for as long as possible. Ian Gardiner, co-founder of lastorders.com, commented:

> Our first round was easy. We had a contact in London so we went to him and said that we needed £250,000 and that we could offer a quarter of the business. He said fine. We are currently organising the second round of finance to raise £2.5 million, but we will still retain a majority – just. In our experience it was better to raise a small amount of money in the first instance and then test the concept rather than try to raise a large amount of money at the start.

But the scale and rapidity of your financing rounds will depend entirely on the sector and the business model. According to Rob Hersov, founder of Sportal, 'Some people who have a unique concept or who are working in a less competitive market have the luxury of being able to raise less money than us and develop more slowly. But we're working in such a competitive market that it's all about speed.'

The venture capital investment process

Stage	Entrepreneur	Entrepreneur and venture capital firm	Venture capital firm	Reports
Approaching the venture capital firm/evaluating the business plan	• Appoint advisers • Prepare business plan • Contact venture capital firms		• Review business plan	Business Plan
Initial enquiries and negotiation	• Provide additional information	• Meet to discuss business plan • Build relationship • Negotiate outline terms	• Conduct initial enquiries • Value the business • Consider financing structure	Offer letter
Due diligence		• Liaise with accountants • Liaise with other external consultants	• Initiate external due diligence	Consultants report / Accountants reports
Final negotiation and completion	• Disclose all relevant business information	• Negotiate final terms • Document constitution and voting rights	• Draw up completion documentation	Disclosure letter / Warranties & indemnities / Memorandum & articles of association / Shareholders agreement
Monitoring **EXIT**	• Provide periods management accounts • Communicate regularly with investor/s		• Seat on Board • Monitor investment • Construction input • Involvement in major decisions	Management accounts / Minutes of Board and other meetings

Reproduced by kind permission of the BVCA.

Exit routes

*'Good VCs are pragmatically obsessed with their exit.
They have to be, because their performance
is measured by their return.'*

SUSAN KISH, FOUNDER OF ZURICH'S FIRST TUESDAY

In deciding whether to back you or not, VCs will assess your team's financial experience: they want to see that someone with financial skills and business experience will use their money to generate value. They will also want an exit route – a mechanism and a time for them to have their money back. VCs normally want to have the option of getting out within three to five years. Their desire to find an exit does not reflect their lack of commitment to your business, more the fundamental nature of the venture capital business: the need to reinvest money in new ideas on a continuous basis.

You need to be aware of the possible exit routes. The two main options are a stock-market flotation (an IPO or initial public offering, see IPO, chapter 13) or a trade sale (for example, to a more established player in the sector). Although IPOs get a lot of press coverage, an investor may be frightened off if an entrepreneur suggests that they are set on an IPO. For many companies a trade sale is a more realistic option, and for every one internet IPO there are reported to be eight trade sales. Some VCs also expect a burgeoning secondary market in partially developed internet businesses. But the exit route should not loom too large. This is because investors want to back someone who is interested in generating value rather than cutting and running.

A high forecast growth rate is necessary for an IPO to be

a realistic exit route for the VC. This is because a company showing high returns may be able to launch an IPO when its revenues are around £10 to £15 million, whereas a business with low gross margins may need to grow to perhaps ten times that size before it can consider an IPO.

Things to bear in mind when approaching possible funders

★ People who have money and want to lend it out in order to make more are busy people, so make your initial contact short and snappy. Take care how you present yourself in person. Venture capitalists may not be enthusiastic about someone who arrives in a swanky car and wears a flashy suit.

★ VCs like to see that you have committed some of your (or your family's, or best friend's) money to your project, but it may not be essential. If it is required, it will need to be a meaningful amount in your financial world to convince them that it will make a difference to you (hence the phrase 'hurt money' – it has to be enough to hurt if you lose it).

★ VCs may also assess the commitment of your team by seeing whether you have left your previous jobs to work full-time on the start-up.

★ Offer the funder a total package. 'We made the mistake of being half-merged with our technology partner at the time we were looking for capital,' recalls one entrepreneur, 'but we would have had a much better opportunity if we had merged before seeking capital.'

★ Take care of every relationship you build up. It is good practice anyway, and you never know when you might need them. If you accept the reality that most deals fall through, you should take good care of the capital sources that show an interest in you, and keep them up-to-date, even if they are not working actively on your current transaction. 'After our second transaction fell through, we couldn't very effectively go back to the first one,' an entrepreneur explains, 'because we had basically let the relationship go.'

★ Be prepared for potential investors letting you down or slowing the investment process to a crawl. 'We lined up as many investors as we could muster, knowing that the majority would fall away when it came to writing cheques – the perceived competition also kept the valuation up during negotiations,' says Rupert Lee-Browne, co-founder of eggsbenefit.com.

★ Try to make sure you only talk to the real decision-makers. 'The so-called commitment committee really caught us off guard,' says one entrepreneur. 'We thought the guy we were talking to all along had the authority to do the deal. Talking to the senior vice-president of investment banking sounded pretty good to us. We should have known otherwise, and the fact that we didn't cost us dearly.'

Appendix

Useful advisory sites

bvca.co.uk – information on UK venture capital groups and matchmaking

evca.com – information on European venture capital groups

nvca.com – information on US venture capital

firsttuesday.com – informal internet club for start-ups

e-start.com – one-stop source of business services and ideas for start-ups

dcfor.com – community site for dot.coms

ukbi.co.uk – information on incubators

digitalpeople.org – forum for entrepreneurs and venture capitalists

Business Angels

The BVCA (bvca.co.uk) publishes a directory of business angels

National Business Angels Network (formerly National LINC – Local Investment Networking Company): nationalbusinessangels.co.uk (020 7329 4141 is the hotline for an information pack)

LEntA Ventures (020 7236 3000)

Beer & Partners: beerprt.com (01306 742104)

VCR (Venture Capital Report): vcr1978.com (01865 784411). The directory costs £295 but can also be consulted at business libraries. The directory is also available on CD-Rom, which makes selecting appropriate VCs easier.

Incubators

Bain: bainlab.com (020 7484 9477)
McKinsey: atmckinsey.com (020 7839 8040)
A.T.Kearney: atkearney.com (020 7468 8000)
Boston Consulting Group: bcgweblab.com (020 7753 5353)
Booz Allen & Hamilton: bah.com (020 7393 3333)
Deloitte Touche: deloitte.co.uk/ebusiness/ (020 7936 3000)
Andersen Consulting: ac.com (020 7844 4000)
KPMG: kpmg.co.uk (020 7311 1000)
Price Waterhouse Coopers: pwcglobal.com (020 7583 5000)
Ernst & Young: eyuk.com (020 7951 2000)
Hawkpoint/LEK: Ideashed (020 7665 4730)

Business school incubators

LBS (020 7535 8805)
Cranfield (01234 751122)

Specialist incubator/funding groups

Amadeus Capital: amadeuscapital.com (020 7298 6800)

Atlas Venture: atlasventure.com – international technology fund

GeoCapital Partners: geocapital.com

Kennet Capital: kennetcapital.com

Crescendo Ventures: crescendoventures.com

European Digital Partners (US$100m fund from KKR)

eVentures – joint venture between ePartners (News Corp) and Softbank (020 7881 2700)

Carlyle Internet Partners (020 7802 8900), run by QXL founder Tim Jackson

Arts Alliance: artsalliance.co.uk (020 7594 4026)

Zouk Group

Global Retail Partners

Gilde IT Fund: gilde.nl (00 31 219 2525)

Vesta Capital (020 7292 0650)

Europ@web (00 331 4413 2222)

Brainspark: brainspark.com

Dawnay Day Lander: D2L.com – sponsored by Andersens, BBC and Colt

business-incubator.com – web development consultancy from Oracle, Cisco, Sun Microsystems and Exodus

uglyducklings.co.uk – technology consultancy from Compaq, Dcfor and Exodus

Springboard Venture Managers

Siliconwharf: siliconwharf.com (020 7922 5166)

AIM-based internet investment funds

Convergence Holdings
e-prime financial
E-Capital
Eurovcstech
EVestment
Internet Indirect
Interregnum
Jellyworks
Magic Moments
MediaInvest
netvest.com
NewCapital Invest
New Media Spark
Oxygen Holdings
Property Internet
start IT.com
Underwriting & Subscription
Virtual Internet.net

Internet incubators

fastfuture.com
eSouk.com
innovationfactory.com
i-cocoon.com
antfactory.com
bizzbuild.com

Sites which match entrepreneurs to VC or angel money

garage.com
matchco.co.uk – new matching service, but you pay £1,000 for advice
ventureseek.com
fourleaf.com
angelmoney.com
be-your-own-boss.com
workz.com
venturedome.com
venturesite.co.uk

Other funders

govgrants.com
Regional grants – contact regional offices of the DTI
DTI: dti.gov.uk (0207 215 5000)
Prince's Trust (0207 707 4001)

CHAPTER 7
Marketing

'You have to have a decent marketing strategy if you are a B2C or you are dead in the water.'

PAUL VICKERY, 3i

'In starting, managing and growing a business online, the focus must be on customer, customer, customer . . . Customers have a bigger voice online. If we make a customer unhappy they can tell thousands of people. Likewise, if you make a customer happy, they can also tell thousands of people. With that kind of megaphone in the hands of every individual customer, you had better be a customer-centric company.'

JEFF BEZOS, AMAZON

'In today's business environment, where customers have information at their fingertips and the cost of switching vendors or suppliers is practically nil, a loyal customer base is a company's most precious and valuable asset. Some customers come and go, but loyal customers are for life. In the end, the customer's experience is a company's brand.'

VANTIVE

'Many people underestimate the marketing costs. It's cheap to get a site up, but it costs a lot to get people to come to the site because it's so competitive.'

CHRIS FROST, FOUNDER ONSENIORS.COM

'It's the customer, stupid!'

PATRICIA SEYBOLD, AUTHOR OF *CUSTOMERS.COM*

What is marketing?

Marketing is about shaping your product to appeal to your target customers, and selling it to them. It involves determining the exact form your product should take, how it would be most effectively packaged and priced, where it would be best sold, and how you should best tell your customers about it and persuade them to buy it.

All businesses need a marketing strategy, and of course web businesses are no exception. In fact, in terms of advertising spend, web businesses have recently been some of the biggest spenders. Notably these have been B2C businesses, and in general B2Cs will need to spend heavily on marketing in order to establish a brand. By contrast, B2Bs often have far fewer customers, which means they can be reached directly without the need for expensive mass media advertising or promotional campaigns.

Web businesses need to heed the general principles of marketing, but there are also internet-specific marketing issues.

How marketing interacts with the product/service

'My advice to would-be start-up entrepreneurs is to remember that the twentieth century was the century of form over content, and it doesn't look like we'll be turning back time on this one.'

DOT.COM ENTREPRENEUR

Form over content

The 'look and feel' of the content of the product or service, the connotations of the name or the brand, and the explicit links made to other products/services or brands is at least as important in the decision-making process of the consumer as the actual content you are offering, and often is much more so. The web highlights the importance of form over content because the customer interacts with your company in a limited way: all they see is your domain name, or the links to your site, and then your site itself with its adverts and links.

Furthermore, each customer sees pretty much the same thing: there may be fewer points of difference between the experiences of your customers than an offline shop can have. For although each customer can view your pages in a different order from other users, click to view different products and even view them differently by zooming or spinning them, these options are far fewer than the whole range of sight, sound, personal contact and other stimuli you experience in a physical shop.

Things do, of course, get more complicated when your site incorporates features such as call backs (see Design, chapter 8) and also when you get to the fulfilment of your product/service. It is at this stage that the politeness of the delivery staff or the efficiency of your credit card payment capturing system adds more layers of complexity to the buying experience.

But, crucially, customers cannot judge how your business will perform in these areas in advance of their purchase. This contrasts with customers' ability to judge in advance whether or not they will be able to catch a taxi from outside a physical shop or be able to park their car outside it. This means that while fulfilment issues are important to customers, for their first purchase they cannot judge how you will perform. Thus, only the credibility of fulfilment promises affects the first purchase, while the actual performance of fulfilment affects only subsequent purchases.

Form is content

And yet, operating businesses on the net collapses the distinction between form and content, because the form *is* the content until the goods are received. This means that the design of your web site should vary according to the characteristics of your target group, so you need to know who they are and what they like. If amazon.com does not end up ruling the internet, it will be because kids don't want to shop where their grandparents shop (and vice versa).

A classic example of a company which mistook its target and so hit off-beam with its marketing is smile.com, the Co-op's online bank. Smile thought its target group would be young, cool, 20- to 30-year-old professionals who wanted internet excitement in their banking life, and so it designed a marketing strategy to appeal to them. In fact, their main customer base has been staid 30- to 60-year-olds who switch money between accounts in order to capitalise on better rates. In retrospect, this is not surprising: few youngsters have much spare cash to invest. The extra spend on Smile's funky marketing may therefore have been money wasted, and, indeed, may have put off some people who were good potential customers.

The web puts customers in charge

The web has changed the balance of power between the company and the consumer. Before the days of online shopping, companies could rely on the difficulties of shopping to keep customers loyal. Many high-street brands thrived on the basis that few people would visit three supermarkets to find the cheapest audio tape. Convenience bred loyalty, and 'location, location, location' was the motto.

But with the advent of e-commerce, customers can check out the options everywhere, and then buy from anywhere. Customers can use comparison sites, or shopping agents, or 'bots' (such as shopsmart.com, or botspot on internet.com) to search the web for a bundle of products and report back which shops are selling them the cheapest. Alternatively, customers can be 'pushed' information by email on cheap deals which suddenly become available, with services such as lastminute.com. Rather than having to visit Thomas Cook or pass its window to find out about reduced breaks next weekend, you can tell lastminute.com that is what you want to hear about and you will get an email telling you what is available.

Customers also have the opportunity in online trading to set their own prices. It's not just auction houses such as QXL.com where this is true. Indeed, if it was, that would hardly be revolutionary, as auctions have been around for centuries. The web has not only enabled constant auctions, it has also brought us services such as priceline.com, which enables customers to set their prices for new products, as opposed to the traditional auction concept of a house clearout. With priceline.com, customers are stating what they would be prepared to pay for a known product or service. It is the equivalent of asking your insurance agent if they would let you know when they have found third party, fire and theft cover for your car for less than £170.

In addition, e-commerce customers can negotiate discounts if they are a group of buyers. Previously, the price of products and services (anything from a telecommunications deal to a short taxi ride) was not negotiable unless you were a corporate purchaser. But now, with services such as LetsBuyIt.co.uk, the internet is creating virtual communities that pool their buying power to negotiate better prices.

Virtual communities have become very powerful things in all manner of areas, from lovers of real ale to stamp collectors. Often the virtual connection leads on to events being organised offline, such as First Tuesday, the meeting place for internet entrepreneurs. Even if the community remains purely online, virtual communities can be as strong as, if not stronger than, many traditional offline communities.

So, with the consumer rendered more powerful by these various means, internet businesses must work hard to sell to the customer, and to retain them. This is what marketing is all about, and this is why marketing is so important to internet businesses.

The principles of marketing

The basic principles of marketing are:

★ work out exactly who your customers are;
★ be rigorous and almost obsessive at working out what they want;
★ work out what you can do to fulfil their wants;
★ put it into practice with the four Ps: product, price, promotion and place.

As the saying goes, 'The customer is king.' Or queen. But it's not always obvious what the customer wants. For example, does Rolex sell watches, an idea of luxury, or the ability to impress people? Does Chanel sell smells, or hope (or perhaps wishful thinking)? You have to specify what your prospective customers want that they do not currently receive, or a way in which they could receive it more cheaply or more conveniently.

Product

For the customer, your product or service has two aspects: its design and its functionality. Both are integral to the customer's conception of the product, and both need marketing. So, Apple Mac advertises the funky design of the i-Macs and the advanced graphics capability they have. For

'You have to offer something online that is better than the offline equivalent.'

DAVID BIRCH, HYPERION

web businesses the design of your product is integrally tied in with, and may even largely mean, the design of your web site. This means you need to ensure that your web design fits in with the conception of your product/service (see Design, chapter 8), and that the functionality of your web site is not of a lower technological level than the functionality of your product/service.

Price

Some have argued that the internet is, or will become, the all-time price leveller. While this assessment ignores the importance of brands and of offline delivery issues, both of which are discussed below, there are important price issues the coming of e-commerce has raised.

It has become extremely difficult to know how to price things sold using the internet because it has spawned a give-away culture. The principle of the 'loss leader' which shops have been fond of to attract customers to buy other products has been expanded by businesses on the net. Many web businesses now offer free products or services, simply in order to build up their potential customer base.

The internet may allow you to have lower costs than offline businesses, which means that your web business may make money while beating the offline competition on price. But the internet also makes competition more complex. An example is the advent of 'co-opetition', a word coined by Intel's Andy Grove. It means that businesses which are in competition offline can become partners online. So, firstresort.com is 25% owned by Thomson, but it sells holidays from all suppliers, not just from Thomson. This helps to make pricing more transparent, because products are presented in a comparable way in a single place.

Promotion

Promoting a product/service is vital if the business is going to grow, because customers cannot buy a product or a service if they don't know about it. As Dan Geoghegan, an e-commerce strategist at HMV, says, 'It is easy to sell something on the net. All you have to do is put up a site, and someone will take a punt and buy your product. The difficulty is getting lots of people to do so.'

Promotion is achieved using PR (public relations), paid advertising of the product/service, and by building the brand over time.

What is a brand?

Communications from a business to a consumer aim to convey positive ideas about that business's product or service, such as quality or value. The kernel of these ideas is known as the product's brand. It takes a great deal of money to build up an effective brand, but a brand serves important functions for both buyers and sellers. Customers have a use for brands because they do not have unlimited time to inform themselves about the features and benefits of all the products and services they buy. A familiar brand reassures the customer that the product or service has certain qualities. The customer is willing to pay extra for this reassurance, which means that the seller derives an advantage from the brand: they can charge higher prices.

Even though brands provide these useful short-cuts for buyers by telling them concisely what the core activities/strengths/beliefs of a business are, many argue that brands are not so relevant in the internet age, because information about a competitor's offer is only a click away. However, things are turning out somewhat differently: in e-

'[The internet] business is all about customer acquisition costs.'

MICHAEL ROSS,
FOUNDER OF
EASYSHOP.COM.

commerce, brands are critical because the company and the product or service is usually invisible. Moreover, although it is easier to reach competitors online than offline, buying habits tend to develop on the net just as they do offline.

How to build a brand

For most businesses, the brand begins with the name. The difficulty for new web businesses is that pretty much all good names are taken, but you should still aim to have a reasonably short name, and maybe encapsulate something of your business in the name. Non-referential names such as the *Evening Standard*'s recruitment business, bigbluedog.com, are a dubious proposition, although Yahoo! doesn't seem to be doing too badly with a name whose meaning is not obvious.

Brands are built through promotion, and because brands are critical for internet businesses, particularly B2Cs, net businesses spend prodigiously on advertising and PR. Forrester Research has estimated that almost half of all money spent by European e-commerce operations is spent on marketing and advertising. 'I don't want to make any profit this year because every dollar I spend on marketing comes back tenfold next year,' is a common refrain from dot.com entrepreneurs.

Online versus offline

What forms of promotion are relevant to an internet business? Almost all of them. The options include both online and offline promotion. The latter category includes both above-the-line and below-the-line promotion.

In a marketing context, above-the-line means traditional media such as television, radio, press and magazines (it means something else in an accounting context). Below-the-line means newer techniques, such as point-of-sale, sales promotions and direct mail. Anecdotal evidence from several quarters suggests that radio is a highly effective way to reach committed 'netizens', because many listen while they surf.

Some web companies argue that they need to advertise offline to build up consumer awareness of their brands. According to Russ Ackerman, the marketing director of BOL, 'it's difficult to create a brand entirely online. Online advertising drives traffic to the site, but it can't create a world-class brand.' For Alice Wenner of handbag.com, 'at the moment the internet audience is too fragmented; you need a whole range of media'. These companies maintain that offline brand advertising increases the effectiveness of online spending – improving click-through rates, for example.

A few web companies, such as boo.com, have promoted their brands before their site was available. But this approach has received a mixed response from industry commentators like Richard Lord, editor of *Revolution*: 'All that money spent plastering the name over billboards only for people who visited the site to find that it wasn't there yet. Maybe this is some clever guerrilla marketing tactic for building suspense which is just too trendy for the likes of me to understand. But I doubt it.'

Other web companies have made a success of concentrating their spending online. Streets Online, which sells books and music, has concentrated on online promotions and is one the UK's top 50 sites. Some start-ups have made a virtue out of their poverty and argue that awareness of a site, particularly in the early stages, can be built without the need for heavy offline spending. Ian Gardiner, co-founder of lastorders.com, says, 'I'm not convinced that offline ads or

'Only 8% to 12% of amazon.com's ad spend is online and the rest is offline. Why is this so? Because people currently spend an average of twenty minutes a day online, whereas they spend an average of five hours a day watching TV.'

TONY RYAN, DELOITTE TOUCHE

'Massive customer acquisition can only be achieved by offline promotions and advertising, not through online routes.'

MARK HOLMES, FOUNDER OF SPACE2.COM

'Online ads only appeal to people who are already online and willing to click. We do direct marketing online and advertising offline.'

ALEXANDER BROICH, BOL

television campaigns are money well spent for a dot.com business. If you pass a poster advertising a web site, are you really going to run home and switch on your PC?'

According to Chris Frost, founder of onseniors.com, a site for the older generation of netizens known as 'silver surfers', 'We're going for the grassroots approach rather than shouting from the rooftops. It's not our job to get people on to the internet. We're targeting small clubs and communities – charities, bowling clubs and needle-craft societies – that already have web sites and we pay 15p per person that gets sent to our site.'

It all depends on your target audience. If you are operating in a mass consumer market, then you will probably eventually need offline mass advertising. If you have a specialised, tightly defined potential audience, you may be able to concentrate your resources on trade magazines and other web sites. For example, if you are a specialist financial services company, your best strategy might be to concentrate on moneyworld.com and ft.com.

For many companies a combination of on- and offline will be necessary. According to Jamie Estrin of Profero, who designed a combined campaign for eXchange holdings, 'The offline campaign aims to introduce the service to internet novices; but for online we're targeting the literate user with the USP – in this case the benefits of comparative financial information.'

PR

The function of public relations is to boost the good and suppress the bad. It can do wonderful things for your product. For example, eBay.com's founders boasted that they spent no money on advertising apart from PR for two years. According to Pierre Omidyar, eBay chairman, 'advertising is not necessarily the most effective way of building a solid group of users. We're more interested in reaching out to people through grassroots efforts. We'll build the site by listening to the community. If you advertise a lot before building your business, that's just shouting from the rooftops.'

How much is enough?

Both online and offline companies are spending heavily on online promotion (see chart). Amazon.com seems to rule the world in web links. But although online promotional spending is set to sky-rocket (increasing from £7 million in 1997 to £50 million in 1999, and rising to £479 million in 2002 according to Fletcher Research), TV will remain the most popular advertising medium (in terms of money spent) in 2004, followed by other categories such as direct mail, press ads and telesales. Fletcher forecasts that online advertising's share of the overall advertising cake will rise from around 7% today to 14% in 2002.

Top UK web advertisers in 1999

Ranking	Advertiser	Spend in £
1	BT	870,000
2	IBM	810,000
3	Bertelsmann	760,000
4	Amazon	750,000
5	Microsoft	720,000

6	QXL	710,000
7=	BA	540,000
7=	Hewlett Packard	540.000
9	Lastminute	490,000
10	United News	470,000

Source: Fletcher Research

These figures give some idea of the budgets of big B2C web sites. More modest sites will not be able to afford these huge sums, but will still have to budget for substantial spending. For example, Onseniors expects to spend about £80,000 a month on promotion (across all media) after its second round of financing. Some sites may choose to spend much more, but a focused B2B site may be able to spend much less.

Place (Distribution)

With any retail internet business, fulfilment is a key issue. This means delivering the product/service satisfactorily and delivering good customer service, not just to one customer but possibly to millions of customers. Many believe that establishing the fulfilment infrastructure for your business is one of the hardest tasks of an internet start-up. It is hard because the systems, such as warehousing and delivery, cannot easily be bought off the shelf. As Richard Lord, editor of *Revolution*, says, 'It wasn't only the idea that made lastminute.com take off, it was that as a start-up they were brilliant because they realised it was all about customer service.'

As we have seen, e-commerce enables the customer to be in charge of the purchase process because the web can dispose of many or even all of the links in the supply chain between the producer and the customer. But with this empowerment comes increased expectations. Customers expect good service to go with the ease of the buying process, and they expect quick action to go with the immediacy of the web. So it is no good having a great web site offering a great product but offering to deliver it in two weeks with confirmation by telephone needed. (Mind you, Dell seems to get away with it!)

Mark Holmes, founder of space2.com, was astonished and mortified when he found he was unable to offer his customers anything better than 48-hour delivery, with no deliveries in the evenings or at weekends. He says: 'We are going to have to bring those guys into the twenty-first century kicking and screaming. There is a huge delivery opportunity out there for somebody, but no one wants to take it.'

One of the most exciting promises of the internet is its ability to revolutionise supply chains, but at the moment one of the main problems is making the supply chain work for you well enough and fast enough. It is no coincidence that the sale of CDs proved so successful so quickly, while grocery shopping services were so slow to take off: CDs fit through letter-boxes. The problem of delivery will be solved in different ways in different places: through mail-boxes at the end of drives in the US, through concierges in apartments in Paris, perhaps through local newsagents and petrol stations in the UK. In any case, your VC will certainly want to know how you intend to get around this problem.

Solving these logistical problems, from warehouse

managing to packaging to delivery, requires businesses to build strategic alliances, and finding the right strategic partners will be an extremely important issue for your business. As one VC says, 'No one has done it alone. Not Amazon, not anyone. You need strategic partners, and you need the right ones.' See Growing, chapter 12 for more.

Handling customer enquiries

Delivery logistics is not the end of your worries. You need to have systems in place that enable you to respond to feedback you get from visitors to your site. This means that you need to:

★ Reply to emails quickly. You may quickly find the number you receive becomes too great to cope with in a reasonable call-back time (which would be a maximum of 36 hours), so you may need a contracted third-party service to do this for you (see Growing, chapter 12).
★ Reply to phone calls generated by a number on your web site. As with email responses, you may need to hire a call centre to enable you to do this.
★ Be able to take payment instantly (see Technology, chapter 9).

It is not a good idea to:

★ instruct visitors to your web site that they will have to telephone to see if the particular goods they want are in stock;
★ tell customers to put a cheque in the post (not only will they hate you for asking them, you'll hate them when they don't).

Remember that bad publicity is always more detailed than good publicity. As Nick Hadlow, IT director of SPSS, says, 'People who are happy with their buying experience rarely do anything more than say, "I've used ABC a few times and they seem quite good to me," while disgruntled people write long, detailed rants, quoting consumer laws they claim have been breached by the company.' So if you do give grounds for bad publicity, at least make sure you apologise.

Finally, you must consider where your customers are going to be. If the business is to be European or global, your marketing needs to be tailored to this, and your web site may well need to have different language and currency options. According to Richard Downs, co-founder of iglu.com, 'People say that the internet is a global market, but that's a bit frothy. Will you be able to support a global customer? You have to customise content and personalise it. For us it means providing an Italian skier with something that they want: they like different resorts and they don't want to fly from Stansted!'

What is the best way of marketing yourself on the web?

If you are planning to advertise yourself on other web sites, you will need to research which sites are most appropriate and the level of traffic they carry. *New Media Age* carries a list of the top 100 sites (nma.co.uk). *Revolution* magazine also publishes supplements covering top web sites. However, the lists are not comprehensive and many of the figures are not ABC audited. The nature of your business will determine whether portals or sites of general interest are appropriate places to advertise. It may be much more cost-effective to target small, specialist sites where you can more accurately reach users who might be interested in your products and services. You will need to analyse traffic data carefully to decide whether buying ads is sensible and you need to choose sites appropriate to your business model.

Strategic partnerships

In addition to the strategic partnerships you need to develop in order to make the core of your business function, links from other relevant sites which become strategic marketing partners are often seen as extremely effective. It is increasingly common for companies with potential customers in common to set up bartering arrangements. The investment bank Merrill Lynch estimates that such bartering has led to some creative accounting, and accounts for as much as 15% of total advertising 'revenue'. A further possibility is using co-branded web sites, where partners split the revenues.

But you should be wary of who you link yourself with; you may have to be as strong a brand as Amazon to get away with being linked to sites that have security or other problems. Be wary of sites on which you can advertise for free and which will link to you for free – they may be sites which could damage your brand image.

Email

Many successful internet companies are developing email as a core part of their marketing strategy. Because few first-time visitors to sites make a purchase, a company can use an email address to send potential customers offers that might interest them. Companies have to tempt visitors to leave their email details because they are unlikely to do so spontaneously (see Design, chapter 8). Typical incentives include competitions, discounts and vouchers. Clickmango offers a letter from Joanna Lumley.

The more information you want, the more of an incentive you have to offer. For example, Netscape offered a £10 Amazon token in return for lots of demographic information from IT workers. The campaign worked well, because Netscape was virtually offering cash.

The attraction of email for companies is that it is virtually free compared with up to 26p a letter for traditional direct mail. There is also evidence that the success rate for email marketing is much higher. According to Charles Meaden of Digital Nation, Psion sent out 30,000 emails in one campaign in 1999 and achieved a 7.5% success rate compared with the 2% normal for direct mail. No wonder lastminute.com sends out 350,000 emails a week.

There is a big debate in the internet industry about the effectiveness of HTML emails versus standard text emails. On the one hand, HTML emails can be much snazzier than text messages and can contain many more links to web sites, but they cannot be read by all web users and they can take a long time to download. Moreover, they arrive as attachments, so someone checking on their emails may simply decide not to open it. But whatever kind of email a company chooses to use, it must be aware of the differences between using email effectively and spamming.

Spamming

Most netheads will tell you that you should on no account spam. Spamming means sending out unsolicited emails to usually unwilling customers. Some people get exceptionally upset by spamming: they write long and angry emails about how they applaud the internet for its advancement of free speech, but they do *not* want to hear about your damnable mature aubergine sale. To minimise problems arising from the use of promotional emails, make sure you allow customers to change or remove their email addresses from your database.

You spam at your own risk

For most businesses, spamming is unlikely to be a good idea – indeed, it is very likely to be a bad one – but this is not necessarily the case. You may consider that you will reach some people through spamming whom you could not otherwise reasonably expect to reach on your budget, and who will be interested in your product/service and not care that they were spammed. You might also decide that the people who send you the angry emails would never have bought your product. You might possibly decide that you don't need the co-operation of any search engines. It is just possible these conditions apply to your business – but if they don't, then don't spam.

Search engines

Even though there are numerous sites on the web devoted to telling you the 2,001 secrets of the search engines, the real rule for search engines is simple, and it is this: if you are a

B2B, you shouldn't need search engines; if you are a B2C and you are relying on them, you are in trouble.

This is because most search engines only reach about 10% of the web and because you cannot rely on coming very high up on a list generated by a search engine. Even if your site is highly relevant to the area or topic, other companies may be paying the search engine to be placed higher on the list. However, because the mystique of search engines is still strong, here are some tips:

★ Search engines rely a lot on content when deciding the relevance of your site, so have a lot of it and pack it with goodness, i.e. with terms relevant to your business.
★ Be sure to devise your metatags carefully and precisely to relate closely to your business's functions. Be aware that metatagging rarely works as a marketing tool (people looking for adult sites are rarely content with your tree-hugging convention in Madagascar), and that ambush metatagging is probably illegal (see Legals, chapter 5).
★ Major search engines such as Yahoo! demand that you stick to their instructions scrupulously. If you do not, you will fall into the 66% of business that they reject. Some search engines, such as Altavista, will only look at content from 25 pages. If your site has more pages, you will need multiple addresses and have to submit a different set of 25 pages from each address to get each set considered by the engines.

Banner adverts

There is much debate in the internet world about the effectiveness of banner ads. Banner ads are adverts placed on the web site of another company. The idea is that you place these ads on sites that are likely to be visited by people who might be interested in visiting your site. You pay the other site to place your ad there, and the amount you pay depends on how many people see the ad. This is usually expressed as a CPM – the cost per thousand for a particular web site. A web site that charges £10,000 per banner and guarantees 500,000 impressions has a CPM of £20 (i.e. 10,000 divided by 500).

However, as visitors to web sites have become more used to the web, so the effectiveness of banner ads has declined. The effectiveness of banner ads is usually judged by the 'click-through rate' – the percentage of ad views resulting in a click on the ad. Some financial services ads achieve a click-through rate of well under 1%.

Many advertisers, particularly those in strong bargaining positions, are now trying to pay by results instead of flat CPMs. In other words, they pay either for the number of customers who have clicked through, or pay a commission based on the number of click- throughs that result in an actual purchase.

The effectiveness of banner ads on some sites is so low that some agencies are now pushing much more sophisticated 'media-rich' ads using video or animation to tempt the visitor's mouse. There is some evidence that these gimmicks are effective in the short term, pushing up click-through rates by 7% to 10%. But many commentators are sceptical about whether their effectiveness will last. As Richard Lord, editor of *Revolution*, says, 'If banner ads are a poor b****** standing on Hyde Park Corner, then rich media ads are a poor b****** standing on Hyde Park Corner with a silly hat on.'

Some tips if you intend to have banner ads are:

★ include a click-on button;
★ design the banner so that it takes as little time to download as possible, so you catch more people.

Selling banner ads

If your business model is based on the selling of banner ads then you will experience this aspect of the web from the other end. Even if you just want to make some extra cash out of the thousands of eyeballs viewing your site every day, you will need to sign up with one of the banner ad agencies. Only the very biggest sites are able to sell advertising space for themselves.

The agencies you need to sign up with depend on the volume of traffic you are able to generate. The larger agencies, like doubleclick.com, are only interested in dealing with high-traffic sites, while the small agencies are happy to put banners even on personal homepages. You can also register your site at domo.co.uk, which aims to be a one-stop site for media buyers. But do be sure to get a listing in *BRAD*, the monthly tome which media buyers rely on for rates. The listing is free.

If you are planning that advertising will be an important revenue stream, you will have to forecast your expected revenues from that source. You will need to make several assumptions, including the average monthly number of page impressions per user, the click-through rate, and whether the ads are sold in-house or by third parties. This will enable you to generate a monthly income figure for advertising. You will probably need to bring in someone who has experience of the sector to help you make these assumptions and reduce the amount of guesswork.

Most commission rates are fairly standard – see those listed in the advertising section of yahoo.com for an example. But be warned: in order to get real money from an advert, you need the consumer to click on the banner, and that means that they have left your site. If advertising is meant to be a secondary feature of an e-commerce site, then don't allow the tail to wag the dog.

Viral marketing

A fairly recent buzzword is viral marketing. This means having something on your site, such as a wacky game, that people will not only wish to see but will, crucially, email to their friends. This has been a successful strategy for some businesses, such as Head and Shoulders, who used a game featuring a cartoon Head and Shoulders boy. But beware that many see viral marketing as just another time-wasting novelty, and so far it has proved successful for very few businesses.

According to Jon Bains of the agency Lateral, 'Viral marketing is a very cynical activity. You're relying on the goodwill of people to distribute it and you have to make sure that the message is good and interesting. There's a thin line between marketing stuff and spam.'

Analyse your site traffic

Effective marketing relies on your knowing not only who your target market is, but also who your actual customers are. You need to install equipment so you can analyse who they are, where they are coming from (in terms of links), what products/services they are buying or viewing from which pages, and when they are exiting. You may then find, for example, that 25% of customers exited on page four. You could then set about changing that page or making the purchase line more direct. Furthermore, you can push information or offers out that your customers might be interested in; cash-rich, time-poor people actually value this, rather than seeing it as intrusive. Find out which of your customers are net profitable (i.e. taking into account the value of service provided) so you can work out those you want to attract and those you don't.

You can buy complicated software to calibrate these calculations for you, such as Engage, but most sites should have enough information in cookie form and in their customer databases once they are up and running not to need such software. Moreover, most growing start-ups find they just do not have the time to assess the implications of the figures they can pull off their system, because all their energies are employed in growing the business.

Appendix

Adability.com is a key resource for ad company information
IPA – Institute of Practitioners in Advertising
AA – Advertising Association
CIM – Chartered Institute of Marketing

Trade magazines –

Revolution (Haymarket)
Marketing (Centaur)
Marketing Week (Haymarket)
Campaign (Haymarket)
PR Week (Haymarket)

CHAPTER 8
Design

Reproduced by the kind permission of BVCA

'First impressions count more with clicks than with mortar.'

'It's got to be intuitive for the user. If it's not clear what you do next, then it's a poorly designed site.'

NEIL CROFTS, HEAD OF EUROPEAN STRATEGY, RAZORFISH

Introduction

It is most likely that you will employ someone else to design your web site: indeed, unless your background is in the area of web design, you almost certainly should do so. But ideally you should work closely with the designer to devise the image and functionality of your web site, since it is the first, and possibly only, thing people will see about your business. This means you need to know some of the tricks of the design trade for attracting people to your site, and then making them buy your product/service if only so that you know which tricks you want the design company you employ to put up your business's sleeve. This chapter cannot turn you into Viant or Razorfish (two of the best-known web services consultancies) overnight, but it may be able to prevent you looking a complete ignoramus when you talk to people in the industry.

The design of your web site and your product must be complementary. Both must grow out of your business strategy and marketing strategy and both must be tailored to appeal to your expected customer base. This means that your designers must also work closely with your technologists in order to ensure that the web site architecture and design is appropriate to your targeted customers, and that it functions well. You should focus on the major design decisions, such as whether royal blue or luminous orange is the right look to appeal to your customers, but you also need to be aware of details, such as ensuring that the site appears similarly on different browsers and that it can be downloaded quickly.

It may sound obvious, but it is worth saying anyway: as part of your general preparation for setting up your site and your business, spend time surfing. The range of different

'If you're really the first player with a new idea that's going to take the market by storm, then you can get away with poor functionality on your site and imperfect customer service. But if you're not sufficiently differentiated – and most sites aren't – then no way.'

NEIL CROFTS, HEAD OF
EUROPEAN STRATEGY,
RAZORFISH

approaches to web site design is broad, as is the variation in quality. Be a magpie: pick the best from everything you see. Ask your colleagues and friends what sites they like, and which ones they hate. This may be the least stressful part of your preparation, and it may also be the most valuable.

Web design

Choosing a designer

The provision of internet infrastructure and services is a highly popular and profitable business. Providing services such as web site design has proved particularly popular and profitable. There are hundreds of such companies in London alone, and certainly thousands around the world. These range from large, well-known companies such as Razorfish and Viant to small boutiques and individuals who offer their web design services on the internet. Choosing between them is a difficult but important decision, because it could significantly affect the success of your business.

Your web site design should grow out of, and continue to be linked to, your marketing strategy. This means that your designers must be in close contact with your marketing team so that what is projected about your business in your advertising and PR campaigns is consistent with the 'look and feel' of your web site.

The marketing people in internet start-ups are tasked with assessing proposals and quotes from different design companies. You may be able to call upon other contacts to help you make a decision, and it is worth contacting previous clients of designers for references. You should probably hold a 'beauty parade', in which you compare the different service/price packages of the various service providers.

What is your site trying to achieve?

The chances are that you will be trying to get visitors to your site to buy something or to carry out some sort of transaction. But it could be that you just want them to hang around for as long as possible. Maybe you plan to sell advertising, or maybe you want to build up a community.

Venture capital firms are somewhat wary of business plans that refer vaguely to revenues being generated wholly or mainly by advertising. But even if that is not your main source of revenue, it could in time be a useful add-on, so do not neglect the need to build as much traffic as possible.

Building traffic is about offering great content in a way that is pleasing to the eye (and the ear, perhaps), and making the total visitor experience as pleasant and easy as possible. Design plays a big role in this.

Designing your site to turn browsers into buyers

'This job involves everything from traditional business practices mixed with the art of visual communications, but the most important job is trying to guarantee that browsers become buyers.'

KARL O'HANLON, VICE-PRESIDENT OF BOO.COM

It is perhaps a little cruel to quote Karl O'Hanlon (see margin) in this context, because boo.com's web site came in for a huge amount of criticism when it launched – to the extent that 'boo-baiting' seemed to become the main sport of internet journalists for the following few months. Boo.com was a heavily hyped fashion retailing site; it launched five months late, suffered from bugs, and gave many users a bad experience. More recently it has been praised for being adventurous (if not successful), and at the time of writing the jury is out.

'Boo.com's marketing has been brilliant, but what they actually publish is very poor, in that it is very difficult to buy anything from their site.'

PAUL GILL,
ALOUD.COM

Even if Boo didn't get it right, O'Hanlon's comment is correct: a cardinal rule of e-commerce is that in designing your web site you should ensure that it is always easy and obvious for people to do what you want them to do, wherever they are in the site and whenever they decide they want to do it. Your site should be structured so that people who visit it are directed towards the end you seek – your MIA. This is not missing in action, but most important action.

What is your MIA? Do you want your visitors to:

★ Buy a computer?
★ Register their details and tell you when they want to travel to New York, or what car they are trying to sell?

THE INTERNET START-UP BIBLE

★ Simply read your content so as to make them spend more time looking at the adverts on your site, or in order to build your brand (for example, bbc.co.uk)?

You may well also have an NMIA (next most important action). While your first choice may be to have someone buy a weekend break to Paris leaving tonight, you need to be prepared for the fact that they might decline your generous offer. In this scenario, if you have the facility for them to register to be sent all your last-minute deals for city breaks or to be sent your weekly newsletter, then you have established an important point of contact and you can now 'push' deals at them at a later date. This is clearly better than making customers 'pull' information from you, which requires them to take action to request information. You need to consider providing incentives to encourage people to leave their email details (see Marketing, chapter 7).

Searching and ordering

There are also several practical tips for encouraging browsers to buy. If your site offers many different goods or services, you need to make it very easy for people to search. That means you have to think of the likely criteria customers might want to search under: for example, size, colour and material for clothes. The searching, just like the navigation, has to be as clear to the first-time user as it is to the site veteran.

It is also important to make it easy for visitors to key in credit card details. According to Jupiter Communications, more than a quarter of online purchases are abandoned because consumers get fed up with keying in credit card and address details. This is why some sites have developed one-click ordering, so that once you have made your selection you can simply click on an icon that has stored your details from a previous transaction.

In addition, you should allow visitors to print off an order form to give them the option of faxing or posting an order. This might seem an odd idea, but some of the biggest US web retailers still find that almost half their orders come in over the telephone from people who have used the web to find out information about goods or services but feel happier about placing an order in a more traditional way. If you don't offer these options, you may lose the orders.

But remember: many entrepreneurs caution against including features which make your site hard to navigate and understand, and the old adage always applies: KISS (Keep It Simple, Stupid!).

> *'The best thing is to make your site clear and uncluttered . . . and from the moment the person arrives at the site, they have to see something relevant to their needs.'*
>
> MATTHEW CRITICO, DOMINO SYSTEMS

> *'Forget fancy technology – have the simplest possible site you can. Don't become another boo.com.'*
>
> RUPERT LEE-BROWNE, FOUNDER OF EGGSBENEFIT.COM

> *'A web site is a piece of communication. Ease of use is the key . . . If I find that it impedes me buying or finding out information, then it's not well designed.'*
>
> MARK ELLIS – REDWOOD NEW MEDIA

Create 'stickiness'

There is general agreement that sites need to be 'sticky', which is to say their design and content should encourage visitors to hang around and return often, thus increasing the chances of turning a browser into a buyer. There are many different ways to skin this particular cat, and some alternatives are hotly debated. One such debate is between the concepts of 'nesting' and 'leaving doors open'.

Some e-commerce sites attempt to lock people in by 'nesting' pages within pages. The idea is that if you make it difficult for visitors to find their way out of the site, they will surely end up buying something.

Other people argue that this runs counter to the very increases in convenience and customer power that web users expect. These people argue that your site should not only have clear and easy navigation towards purchasing or registering for your product/service (i.e. your MIA), but also that you should always show clear exit points. As Dan Geoghegan, responsible for HMV's e-commerce policy, says, 'If you look at Yahoo!'s site you'll see about 20 different ways to exit from every page. The best way to keep customers is always to show them where the door is.'

The most popular way to encourage visitors to remain at a site is to provide information in which they may be interested. You need to think carefully about what a potential visitor to your site might like to know. British Airways puts much more than its schedules and ticket prices on its site; there is a wealth of information about destinations as well. Iglu provides snow reports. Amazon provides reviews of and recommendations on its books. Share trading sites offer not just share prices but also financial news and analysis. The idea behind this approach is that if a site is too commercial, too much of a pure hard sell, it may put visitors off.

Another route is to develop the interactivity of your site. This approach is particularly favoured by 'community' sites. You can offer chat rooms, question boards and experts to tempt potential customers to extend their visit. These features may tempt visitors back to the site as much as the products and services on offer. According to Maxine Benson, co-founder of Everywoman, 'We saw a genuine need for a community site where women who had a business or who were in business could find information, exchange ideas and pool or barter talents.' This may not sound like a very commercial proposition, but some community sites are now being recognised as having huge commercial value because they are a way of reaching valuable groups of customers. For example, Unilever recently put $200 million into a joint venture with ivillage.com, a US women's portal and community site.

Another common technique is to entertain the visitor. The entertainment can take the form of games, cartoons and other graphics, although this approach may be much better suited to some sites than others. This is the point where the boundary between design and marketing starts to blur. According to Alex Czajkovski, marketing director of QXL, 'We do everything we can to make the web site fun. The whole experience should be a fun, interactive process.' Lastminute.com adopts the same approach: 'We've added a lot of fun elements. It's a way of showing that we're not just a booking engine.' The big risk with providing high-tech entertainment, however, is that it slows the downloading of your site, particularly for users with less recent technology.

An alternative way to make your site 'sticky' is to encourage repeat visits by providing an incentive for returning, such as reward points. Obviously, incentive systems must fit in with your target market and the strategy of your business. For example, an incentive reward point system may be appropriate for a student dating service, but not for Harrods.

Build in methods of increasing customer contact

The technological 'back end' of your site should be built to capture and use all customer data you receive (see Technology, chapter 9). There are also systems that enable you to increase the amount of customer information you receive by encouraging customer contact.

One method is to offer to call a customer using a 'voice over IP' system, such as netcall.com. With this system a customer hits a button on your site to register that they would like to be called back by you to discuss your product/service in greater detail. Netcall logs the caller's request and directs the call to a call centre. Customers can choose to be called back straight away or at any other time they specify. Businesses have found that this system greatly increases conversion rates (i.e. the number of customers who actually buy the product or service) compared with the alternative of providing a freephone number. It should also work out cheaper than providing a free telephone number.

Furthermore, such a system provides you with a simple but invaluable piece of information: your customer's telephone number. Once you have this, you have used your web site to convert a cold call into a direct telephone list. (However, beware telephone marketing to consumers at home. Although common in the US, this is still relatively rare in the UK, and many people find it intrusive and rude.)

Allow customers to personalise your site

From the technology that enables people to bookmark sites to the creation of personal shopping baskets, the technology enhancements of the internet are arranging things so that it is the customer not the seller who is in charge. An extension of this process is the idea of allowing customers to personalise your site. On the web the differences in convenience between different sites are not as great as that between shops in the real world, but they do exist and are growing, because customers get used to sites and because they like to personalise sites they visit often. So allow your customers to personalise your site as much as possible to make it user-friendly for themselves, rather than having to fit in with your idea of what makes a great site. The trend to personalise has spread: Yahoo! has My Yahoo!, and Amazon has progressively increased the extent to which users can personalise its site.

Let customers help themselves

Then take things a step further by allowing your customers to combine your products/services, or, if possible, build the product to their own specifications. Alvin Toffler wrote about this over 20 years ago in his book *The Third Wave*. He called it 'pro-sumption' – the meeting of production and consumption. Sites selling computers provide a classic example of this: the best of these enable the customer to build the exact computer they want with the extras they require, not the extras the retailer has negotiated to be bundled into the price.

Altering defaults

One last technical feature of the design of your site that you need to consider is to enable customers to access as many aspects of the functionality and design of your site as their technology will allow. This means that you may need to advise customers how they can alter their default set-up in order to fit in with your site design. See how egg.com resolves this for their customers so that they can recognise the required Verisign certificates:

For Internet Explorer version 4

1. At the toolbar select *View*
2. Select *Internet Options*
3. Select *Content*
4. Click on *Authorities*
5. Scroll across to and tick *Verisign Class 3 and 4*
6. Finally, click on *OK*

For Internet Explorer version 5

1. Select *Internet Options*, via the tools menu or the control panel
2. Select *Content*
3. Click on *Authorities*
4. Scroll across to and tick *Verisign Class 3 and 4*
5. Finally, click on *OK*.

How much does a web site cost?

Asking how much it costs to design and build a web site is like asking 'how long is a piece of string?'. Nevertheless, it is important for planning purposes to have some idea of the costs involved.

It is possible to get a web site up and running very cheaply with the use of online kits. However, these are unlikely to be a viable option for a serious web business. At the other end of the scale, multi national companies are paying millions of pounds to consultants such as Razorfish to design complex sites. Where does this leave the start-up entrepreneur?

Many start-up entrepreneurs are in a good position because they have a relatively simple business idea, which is much easier to translate on to a web site than a complex international business. Several entrepreneurs we spoke to in the course of researching this book had followed the DIY approach and set up web sites themselves, spending a great deal of their own time refining the programmes. However, other companies may lack the skills or time to follow this route.

Most start-ups without huge backing approach small web site design boutiques, which provide cost-effective solutions. According to Fletcher Research, 10% of companies spend £10,000 or less on their web sites, and a further 30% spend between £10,000 and £50,000. An average B2B site with significant ambitions might cost £75,000 to £100,000.

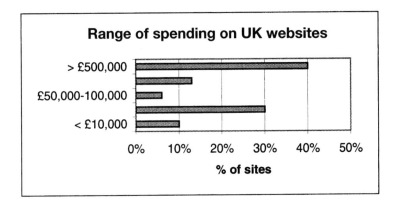

Range of spending on UK websites

Source: Fletcher Research

The cost figures in the bar chart include not just the bill for 'design' – choosing the colours, layout and architecture – which may be a modest part of the total, but also the much more substantial costs of software and technology (see Technology, chapter 9). It's hard to break these costs down because of the differing levels of complexity of sites and the different needs of different entrepreneurs. Some entrepreneurs are confident with technology and programming but need to buy in designers; others are from a marketing and design background and will incur the bulk of their costs on technology.

The major disadvantage of starting out with a very modest site is that it may not be able to grow with the business. As Richard Downs, co-founder of iglu.com, commented, 'We used a small boutique at first, but it was not able to scale up as Iglu grew, so we moved to a bigger design house.' There may be a risk of disruption to the business if it is necessary to take one site down and replace it with another. However, many web businesses mutate as they grow, so it is probably sensible to accept that the web

'You need to design a site that is scaleable and robust enough to take into account expansion of content and likely usage. You can add extra capacity through your web hosting company, but it could be a false economy to build too cheaply.'

MARK ELLIS,
REDWOOD NEW MEDIA

site will need to mutate as well. According to David Birch of Hyperion, a consultancy firm, 'A web site can never be regarded as finished – it's just a series of rolling prototypes.'

As the business grows, it may be necessary to spend much more on designing a robust web site. According to Fletcher Research, 40% of UK transactional web sites cost more than £500,000. As Martin Cheesborough of Quidnunc explained, 'The actual act of putting up a web site need not be expensive at all. But if you want to make it highly robust then that costs a lot more. If it would be very damaging to your business if your web page went wrong, then it is worth paying more. That's when you get into paying £500,000 upwards.'

However, figures about the 'cost' of a web site are confusing because different figures include different things. Some internet service companies offer just design, others just technology, and still others an integrated service (see People, chapter 10). What you pay will depend on what skills you have in-house, your budget, your ambitions and your timescale.

Appendix

Three sets of skills are needed by consultancies who want to help companies (existing as well as start-ups) become 'web-enabled' strategy (optimising the business model, designing an organisation which can make it happen), IT and design.

There are a number of different kinds of firms active in this 'space' (as the Americans call it):

★ Firms claiming to be strong in all the three skill areas:
iXl.com
quidnunc.com
razorfish.com

sapient.com
scient.com
viant.com
★ European pure-plays, such as Icon Media Lab from Scandinavia
★ Design-based firms include Modern Media Poppe Tyson, Amaze, Nvision
★ Design and IT-based firms, such as Oyster
★ IT-led firms: e.g. FI group, Logica
★ Strategy-led groups: e.g. McKinsey, Bain

The Big Five (audit-based consultancies): Andersen Consulting, KPMG, PwC, Ernst & Young (currently selling their management consultancy business to Gemini), Deloitte Touche Ross. These are the big gorillas at the edge of the market: they have strategy and IT skills and are just about the only firms with the armies of IT consultants who can work on the legacy IT systems which run big company payroll and ERP (entreprise resource planning) systems like SAP. Their well-publicised problem is that they are losing staff left, right and centre. They find it hard to hire or retain funky young designers and the young IT people who have grown up with the internet not Cobol and C++.

Sites to consult listing design companies:
revolution.com
newmediage.com

CHAPTER 9
Technology

Reproduced by the kind permission of BVCA

'With e-commerce, the technology is the experience.'

RICHARD DUVALL, CEO OF EGG.COM

*'You don't need to have technological
competence in the founder, but he
or she has to know where to find it.'*

NEIL CROFTS, HEAD OF EUROPEAN STRATEGY, RAZORFISH

Introduction

It goes without saying: e-commerce is a technology business, and your business won't get far if the technology isn't working. According to a recent survey by Andersen Consulting, one quarter of online shopping experiences in the US fail because of technical problems. Having an e-commerce site which crashes is like opening a shop for business, then locking the door.

This doesn't mean that you yourself have to become a full-scale technology geek, but the more you learn yourself, the less you will have to take on trust. This chapter should give you the baseline of technological knowledge you need to start asking the right questions. So, the first step has to be to get yourself educated.

'I can't cut code, but I do know enough to ask the important questions.'

RICHARD DOWNS, CO-FOUNDER IGLU.COM

Get a TLD

Or rather the very first step, and one which you will hopefully have undertaken already, is to get yourself a top-level domain name. This is a prerequisite for any serious e-commerce venture – a web address ending in '.com' or '.net', or, '.co.uk' if you don't want to be global, or the proposed '.eu'. You must have one of these if your ambition is to be taken at all seriously; to try to carry out e-commerce from a Geocities site, or from an address like 'http://www.randomisp.com/pages/widgets.html' is pretty much doomed to failure. You need to act now, and reserve the best domain name you can think of (sadly, 'www.widgets.com' is already taken). Consult Legals, chapter 5 for information on how to go about registering your domain name.

Then get educated

This book will give you the basic knowledge you need, but a business book can't really give a detailed course in web technology. The best place to learn about the technology is on the web itself. Whatever the area of technology you are interested in, there will almost certainly be a 'frequently asked questions' document (an FAQ), and many of these are available online at faqs.org. For more detailed advice, you may want to join a mailing list such as firsttuesday.com, or post a query to a technology-based web site like slashdot.org. There is a huge amount of information on technology available on the web, and you can usually get advice on technical questions for free, if you are prepared to put up with being patronised a bit.

Business decisions and technology decisions

For most of the key technology decisions you need to make in your start-up, the option will be there to pay someone else to do it for you. For most decisions, this option may well be the right one to take, but that doesn't mean you should think of technology as something other people look after.

The reason for this is that, in the web business, a lot of your business decisions are technology decisions in disguise, and vice versa. For example, if you are selling software for download, then without knowing it you have taken the decision to require a lot of dedicated bandwidth. If you are a specialist news site hoping to make money from selling advertising, then whether you know it or not you have taken the technology decision to require 100% uptime or thereabouts, and to need very great flexibility in bandwidth requirements (to handle peaks in demand for your site when there is breaking news).

You also need to consider your prospective customers' technology. If you want to use the latest interactive technology to make your site the best, then you need to be sure your target demographic segment will have the modern computers and high-speed connections to make your site usable. Every time you take a business decision, you have to think, What kind of technology will I need to deliver this? What changes do I need to make to my existing technology? Every time you take a technology decision, you need to think, How does this alter the options available to my business?

The basics: ISPs and servers

An ISP (internet service provider) provides customers and sites with a network connection. A hosting service provides you with a server; consumers only need an ISP (such as Compuserve, Freeserve, etc.), while web companies need a host as well. Your host is almost always your ISP too, unless you are a huge web business. The two services are generally a better deal if they are bundled than if you try to unbundle them and arrange them yourself.

If you are a huge web business, you are probably in the business of owning your own servers, and you will need to sort out a deal with one of the biggest ISPs, or more likely with a number of large ISPs. These are called tier 1 NSPs (network service provider), which is to say they are basically telecommunications companies. So, for example, Yahoo! uses a number of ISPs, and all are NSPs. If you are a smaller web business you may also get your hosting from an ISP, but not necessarily a large one. The leading non-ISP hosting companies such as UUNet, BT Net, PSINet, Planet Online, Exodus and Level 3 all have close relationships with big telecommunication companies, but smaller hosting companies are also now emerging.

Choosing your software

Is Microsoft the enemy?

When choosing the software to design your site you will find that the large number of web design programs available today means that you need never go through the tiresome business of learning how to write in HTML. However, there are a few things to be aware of when choosing your design program. A fundamental question is whether to use Microsoft or to avoid it.

Many people in the internet technology community see Microsoft as a rampant, greedy and monopolistic producer of aggressively marketed but poorly designed software, and they pray that Judge Jackson, the US judge overseeing the Microsoft anti-trust case, will forcibly split the company up. Others think there is more than a trace of paranoia in this attitude, and argue that Microsoft has enabled computer technology to penetrate and benefit our lives more rapidly by creating user-friendly standards in many types of software.

Whatever your view, you are likely to have to make a fundamental decision about Microsoft fairly early on. Microsoft products are designed to work well together, and generally work less well with non-Microsoft products. So if you design your site using a Microsoft tool, you may find that it doesn't work properly with a server using non-Microsoft software, or can't be viewed properly in browsers other than Microsoft Internet Explorer, without a few minor changes.

It is a good idea to find out about interesting little nuances like this before you go live, so you should always test your site using a variety of browsers on the server with which you plan to go live, before actually putting the site in front of the public.

Just in case any of the very nice people in Microsoft's legal department are reading this, let us state clearly and without further ado that we are not saying Microsoft fails to implement industry standards. As we understand it, Microsoft claims it does implement standards, and that it does so more fully than others, which may have consequences for compatibility. Microsoft always stresses that it only ever 'extends' standards where functionality is required that is not covered by any existing standard.

While we are on the subject of compatibility, one technologist offers this advice about browsers:

My inclination would be to specify IE and Netscape from, say, version 3 onwards. I have no idea what Mac users use nowadays, but they'll complain whatever you do. And make a point of specifying on your homepage that your site 'works best with' IE version 3 onwards, Netscape Communicator 4.7 and later and Linx 3 for Solaris, or whatever.

Can you **create your site** for free?

The leading web server software is called Apache, which is available free, gratis, for nothing, courtesy of the frighteningly skilled techno-anarchists of the Free Software Foundation, at apache.org. Apache runs on the Linux operating system, a free version of Unix, which is also available free, at linux.org.

Using and installing Linux and Apache is likely to be a shock for someone used to Macs and/or Windows – the 'command-line interface' used makes running programs feel more like 'proper' computer programming than using a graphical operating system. But the lack of fancy graphics means that Linux/Apache is *fast*, and speed is the number one criterion for judging a system whose job is to serve web pages. You will see on the Free Software Foundation's web site, fsf.org, that these techheads consider their software, which is continuously checked and debugged by thousands of brilliant net nerds, as less buggy and therefore less liable to crash than Microsoft software, which is checked by a few hundred Microsoft staff.

'Free' software is, of course, only free if you don't put a value on your own time in using it – for example, if you are a computer hobbyist. The Microsoft solution (Windows NT Server) is much more user-friendly. However, while NT comes with free technical support from Microsoft, this is not such an advantage as it might seem. For one thing, stories of frustration with technical support are legion. For another, the free software community are always willing to answer questions from people who are installing free software for the first time, so long as those people give some appearance of having read the FAQs. Try the Usenet news groups comp.os.linux and comp.sys.apache, or the IRC channels #linux and #apache. But be prepared for some rather patronising individuals, particularly on IRC.

The Free Software Foundation argues that its free software is less 'buggy' than Microsoft's, and also that servers running Linux and Apache have less downtime than comparable Microsoft servers. With all software you have to make compromises between speed, security and stability, and many people like the Linux compromise, believing it to deliver high uptime and to be fast with acceptable security.

Others consider the performance gap between Microsoft and Unix systems, including Linux, to be less wide than hardcore Linux fans will tell you; they will even claim that for some sites Microsoft is faster, although typically it is not. But the key is that Microsoft can often be cheaper in the long run, because it takes less skill to be a webmaster using Microsoft than using Linux.

According to the Free Software Foundation, around 20% of servers run Apache on Linux, around 30% run Apache on a commercial Unix platform (Linux is a form of Unix), while around 40% of servers run Microsoft Windows NT running Microsoft Web Server, or another server package designed to run Microsoft Windows.

Store your pages offline

You may also want to use technologies other than 'static' HTML pages for your site. The current trend in web design is, rather than having the pages stored on the server in the form of HTML files, to have the pages generated 'dynamically' using information stored in a database, using a program which can create an HTML page to order whenever a visitor comes to the site. This might seem like an inefficient way to go about things, but, depending on the nature of your site, it might be the best way to go about it. If, for example, you plan on updating the site very frequently, such as for a news site, then adding items to a database will be much more convenient than coding a new HTML page twenty or thirty times a day.

This sort of 'active server' site is achieved using what is commonly (among geeks) known as CGI scripts. CGI stands for Common Gateway Interface (see cgi101.com). CGI is a good technology name to drop. It enables you to add a counter, a form to let visitors send you mail or place an order, and much more. If you've ever looked at a site such as amazon.com, DejaNews, or Yahoo!, and wondered how they did it . . . the answer is CGI.

Moreover, the only way you can produce a site which can be customised by the customer is by using a database back-end. The names to drop if you think your site should be run on an active server are Perl, Python and ASP. The first two of these are programming languages which extract and process text and layout codes from a database; the third is a specialised all-in-one complete server package from Microsoft.

Again, the usual caveats about mixing Microsoft and non-Microsoft software apply, but ASP is user-friendly for the non-specialist. Of course, if your web site really takes off and has to handle millions of page views and hundreds of updates a day, you may need to have a special dedicated application written for you in a 'proper' programming language like C++.

When buying your webspace – if initially it's going to be on a shared machine – make sure you specify that you'll be expecting to run CGI scripts, and the sort of thing you want to do. They can significantly affect the load on the server. Demon, for instance, severely restricts the sort of CGI scripts you can run on your tenner-a-month account's 30Mb of homepages.

Functionality you need

What else does your web site need on the technology front?

Credit card acceptance

Your site needs to accept, in the words of one e-commerce entrepreneur, 'every kind of plastic going'. Online credit card acceptance is crucial if you are serious about e-commerce. Asking people to send a cheque in the post is inconvenient for them, and works against the 'instantness' of the medium. You will get very few impulse buys if you can't take credit cards. An absolute minimum would be Visa and Mastercard. Ideally, you should add Amex, as well as various debit cards such as Delta or Switch (however, you may find the merchant fees a bit high on Amex in particular, and many successful sites only take the big two credit cards).

Merchant agreements

In order to accept credit card payments, you will either need to have a merchant agreement with Visa and Mastercard, or have your processing done by someone like Kagi (kagi.com), who will process your transactions for a fee. This is not a bad option for a small e-commerce site which is not planning to have the kind of transaction volume which would make a merchant agreement cost-effective. It does, however, give your business a kind of 'small-time' feel, because at the time of writing the technology is such that the customer can always tell, and it is not as convenient for the customer as being able to carry out transaction processing without leaving your site.

Your bank should be able to advise you best on merchant agreements for credit card transactions. For the actual software to carry out credit card transactions over the web, there are several commercial packages available, and a few free ones are being developed. If you decide to hire your web hosting from a service company, they will probably be able to supply you with one of these packages and help you to install it.

Make sure you specify that you will need CNP (card-holder not present) merchant status. Although this may appear obvious, remember that no matter how new to the idea of e-commerce you may consider yourself, you will almost certainly be dealing with a lot of people who know nothing at all, or have misconceptions.

Security

If you are accepting payments over the net, then you need to think about security. This is not only to reassure the customer but also to protect your own business. Customers have proved surprisingly willing to submit their credit card details over the net, once they are used to the concept of using the web, mainly because they know that, in the absence of a signed receipt, the risk of credit card fraud is borne by the card company and the merchant – in other words, by you.

Some credit card issuers are, in the small print, saying that fraudulent internet transactions are nothing to do with them. Consumers may become a little more cautious over time, so it is probably a good idea to:

★ tell the customer that the credit card information is secure because you're using Blowfish, IPSEC or whatever;

★ have a link to a security statement giving a lot more detail (since the web site owner will be buying the secure transaction facility, there should be a ready-cooked statement about security available from the provider, and it won't give away any secrets!).

The industry standard for encryption of credit card details is 128-bit Secure Socket Layer (128-bit SSL). Whatever the transaction-processing solution you decide on, make sure it offers 128-bit SSL. With that you can be pretty sure credit card data submitted to your site will be safe against snoopers and most forms of web pirate.

Of course, if you then decide to leave the data lying around in an unprotected directory on your server, with poor safeguards against unauthorised access, you will probably get all you deserve. Make sure that all such sensitive information is stored in a protected directory, only accessible by your own billing system, and preferably in encrypted form. Security is another topic which could have a whole book dedicated to it; as a start-up entrepreneur, your main priority should be to ask pointed questions, listen to the answers, and make sure that whoever is responsible for the IT side of your business knows that you consider security a top priority. If this is you, then you need to be finding out. Try the previously mentioned net resources.

User tracking

In order to get the most out of being a web entrepreneur, you should be using your site to learn about your customers while you are selling to them, so that you can tailor your offerings to their needs. To do this, first you will need to get information about them, then store it, and then relate the information to the users when they visit your site again. There are many ways to achieve this but the best one is to use cookies.

Cookies

A 'cookie' is a small file deposited on the hard disk of visitors' computers whenever they visit your site. If you have cookies set up on your site, your server will be able to read the cookie file when the visitor returns, and to associate the information in the cookie with the information in your customer database. So the cookie might contain a customer's name, type of computer, the password they chose for your secure server (in encrypted form, of course), and other information that would otherwise have to be laboriously typed in every time the customer returned.

It is particularly useful to store passwords in a cookie file, as this means that customers only have to identify themselves to you once, which increases convenience at a small cost in security. Of course, the cookie file only really tells you that it is Mrs Jones's computer visiting your site, not necessarily Mrs Jones herself. Don't make your cookies larger than they have to be; most of the information about a customer, such as purchase records, should be on your own database, so that you don't need to wait until Mrs Jones returns to the site before you can devise a marketing plan for her.

Cookies are easiest to use in conjunction with a database-driven, active site, but dedicated cookie servers can be used for any kind of site. Other means of customer tracking, and certainly anything which requires the customer to install an executable program on their local computer, are generally frowned upon as being excessively invasive of privacy, and a great way to spread viruses to boot. Use these methods if you have powerful reasons for doing so, but don't be surprised if less than 20% of your customers agree to accept your tracking program on their system. Some die-hard privacy enthusiasts will reject your cookies too, but this is increasingly rare. These hardy souls will just have to put up with typing their passwords in every time they visit your site.

Privacy of data

Obviously, if you are storing personal data about your customers on your site, they will have a legitimate interest in what is going to happen to that data. In the UK and much of Europe, there are laws on data protection with which you have to comply (see Legals, Chapter 5). And more generally, failing to keep personal data secure, or being too promiscuous about sharing it with other sites, will tend to get you a bad reputation on the net.

Your site should have a 'privacy statement', which only needs to be a single HTML page, but which should be accessible from your front page to reassure the nervous. In it, you should detail the kind of encryption you are using on stored customer data, the kind of uses you will and will not put that data to, and information about how a customer can change or remove the information you hold about them. Check out the privacy statements of some sites you respect.

'Bells and Whistles'

One of the key technology decisions which is also a business decision is about what kind of elements you will have on your site: whether you will stick with standard HTML, or whether your site will use all the 'extensions' software companies have made available, like Shockwave, Java and VRML. There are advantages and disadvantages to both alternatives.

On the one hand, staying with HTML means that your site will be stuck with words and pictures – not necessarily a bad thing if the site is well designed, but not as much fun as having animations, interactive games, live chat and all the other features the web makes possible. On the other hand, every non-standard 'plug-in' program you require the user to have installed as part of their browser reduces the number of people who will be able to use your site to its full potential.

Note also that HTML is WAP-enableable. WAP means wireless application protocol, and WAP-enableable means that the data can be accessed from a mobile phone. The rule is that text can be, graphics can't. Not yet, anyway.

In particular, many people would advise against making any advanced non-standard features into essential parts of the ordering process for an e-commerce site. The example of boo.com is a cautionary one here: it was a good idea to use Shockwave Flash to allow customers to try out different combinations of sportswear, but a somewhat worse idea to have the site set up so that you needed an advanced computer and all the latest add-on programs to buy a pair of shoes. If you are thinking of using features on your site which depend on an add-in, then consider whether the people who do not have it are likely to be customers of yours.

A lot of sites allow access to versions without the bells and whistles. It means a little more coding, but can make a big difference to usability. For example, someone using a 'heavy' web site through a corporate internet connection may find performance perfectly acceptable, but the same person using a personal connection through a modem link at home might be grateful for the ability to select a text-only or 'flash-free' version.

You should also think about whether using add-ins will compromise the security of your site. Many plug-ins, such as Java, have a tendency to allow outsiders access to bits of your server.

Advertising

There are two technological issues concerned with advertising on your site:

★ If you are intending to have banner adverts you need to build your site around the space where they will go, because banner adverts are a fixed size. If the space you leave is too small, then no banner ads.
★ You must ensure that banner ads (or any other links or

ads on your site) open up a new window when they are clicked upon. Otherwise you have just given up your customer and they will have to actively choose to come back to you, rather than defaulting back to you when they finish with the site you advertised or linked to.

Hosting

Unless you are really serious about being in the web site hosting business, or unless you have really big ambitions (and a budget to match), you will probably at least want to start off having your site hosted on servers owned by somebody else. This doesn't mean that you won't want a top-level domain, just that you won't be the owner of the physical servers on which your site resides. Many quite big e-businesses don't own their own servers, and from the customer's point of view there is absolutely no difference between pages held on servers you own, or pages on a hosted server.

Being your own host

It is hard to resist the temptation to say that if you have to ask what to do to run your own server, then perhaps you had better not. This is too pessimistic, however; it is perfectly possible for a novice to learn how to set up and run a web server, but it will involve assiduous reading of the FAQs and manuals, a fair amount of time spent online asking for help, and, probably, paying for some specialist help at times.

Running your own server is not necessarily the cheap way to establish a web presence – the specialist hosting companies have the advantage of economies of scale. But it does give you more control over your own technology, and it gives you much more flexibility: you can upgrade the technology when your site needs it, and not when the host decides to, and you will be able to choose your own software.

If you have a degree of technical competence, or the enthusiasm to learn, it is an option you could consider, as long as you're not too addicted to getting any sleep. If your web site serves private individuals, it will (hopefully) get used heavily at weekends, at night and first thing in the morning before people go to work, as well as during normal working hours. Therefore, unless you can live with the occasional eight-hour outage, you need to set up the server so it can page or call you if anything goes down.

Who can you buy hosting from?

For companies on very small budgets it is possible to get a free hosted e-commerce system from ait2000.com, which you can link to your web site. The catch is that you have to incorporate ait2000's logo on your shopping cart. So the majority of web companies buy hosting services. It is possible to buy just the basic hosting service or to buy a 'full package', including site design, credit card processing services and lots of add-ons. At the end of this section is a checklist of all the issues you will need to address when buying a web hosting package. But by far the most important questions are those of bandwidth and uptime.

Bandwidth

Bandwidth is a measure of information transfer, and it is the quantity by which web hosting services are usually priced. Bandwidth is measured in megabytes per unit of time, and every time a page is served from your server to a site visitor, it uses some bandwidth. Serving the page takes up some time on your host's CPU (central processing unit), and incurs a telecoms cost, and that's what you are paying for when your hosting service sends you its bill.

In order to work out what the best hosting deal is for you, you'll need to have an idea of what kind of bandwidth you will need. This should be calculable from numbers that you will have calculated for your business plan. The bandwidth you'll require should be equal to the number of pages you intend to be serving (= visits × pages served per visit) multiplied by the average size of one of your pages (which will depend on your site design). You then need to consider whether your page views will be spread out through the day, or concentrated in time. If you expect an average of 5,000 pages served per day, then your bandwidth requirements will be much higher if you think they will all come during one time zone's lunch hour.

You may not need as much bandwidth as you think. Even the largest UK sites are rarely using more than a 45Mb feed, and many do not even reach 10Mb. The best way to decide how much bandwidth you will need is to sit down and discuss things with your hosting company. But bear in mind that they will always try to sell you as much bandwidth as possible, so get a number of quotes, and monitor how much bandwidth you are actually using once the site is up and running.

Beware promises of 'unlimited bandwidth'. Some hosting services will offer you unlimited bandwidth for a flat fee. In point of fact, bandwidth is always limited, by the amount of hardware your host has. More often than not, 'unlimited bandwidth' means 'we don't think any of our customers are going to get very big'. Look at it this way: unlimited bandwidth is a very good thing when it's your site taking up all the bandwidth on your hosting service's computers, and it's not costing you an extra penny; unlimited bandwidth is not such a great thing when someone else is doing the same thing, with the result that nobody (including you) can access your site. This means that you can't get on to your site to say sorry, and your customers can't get on to your site to read that message. Instead they get thrown off your site, or have very, very slow download times that could time out, or they see an error message when attempting to access the site.

A lot of 'unlimited bandwidth' deals are loss leaders. The thing to do is to make sure you have a minimum commitment to bandwidth guaranteed. If you're going to run a promotional campaign, or just because of sudden success, you need to make sure your guaranteed bandwidth can be quickly increased. Ideally, it can be decreased again, so that you only pay for what you need. What you don't want to do is get into a deal where it's going to take 90 days to increase the bandwidth to your site.

If you get thrown off your 'unlimited bandwidth' server because you are chewing up the bandwidth so fast that all the host's clients are jammed, the situation doesn't necessarily just return to normal once service is restored. Your hosting company needs either to increase bandwidth (which could take them some time because they would have to acquire hardware in order to do so) or find and eliminate the problem which is rendering inaccessible all the sites they serve – you. In theory, you could keep these hosts hosting your site and find a new ISP, but it is likely to be a better deal for you to get a hosting deal with an ISP and start paying properly for your bandwidth.

It is true that there are some good operatives who offer 'unlimited bandwidth', but you shouldn't be counting on this for anything other than a small site. In any event, you should certainly ask your hosting service some hard questions about how much total bandwidth they have, and how well placed they are to cope with sudden peaks in demand.

Uptime

The other crucial measure you need to take into account when dealing with your hosting service is the uptime percentage – the percentage of time which your hosting service will promise to keep your site available. In an ideal world, your site would be available twenty-four hours a day and seven days a week – '24/7', in the jargon. However, software crashes, hardware burns out, and power cuts happen. In order to be totally reliable, your hosting service would need multiple back-up systems running in parallel, in multiple remote locations. This costs money, and incremental increases in guaranteed uptime cost more and more as you strive towards the barely attainable goal of 100%. So the first step must be to work out how much uptime you actually need.

It is worth thinking about uptime in terms of the number of days per year you are prepared to put up with having your site inaccessible. For example, 99% uptime implies that your site will be inaccessible for three and a half 24-hour days every year – not all that good, really. Going up to 99.9% uptime would mean that your site would only be down for eight hours in a year, which might be more tolerable. Of course, it would depend how this was distributed, bear in mind that:

★ you must always expect the worst distribution – that your site will crash for an eight-hour block the day after a big PR campaign;
★ downtime is very unlikely ever to be evenly distributed through the year – just as train delays never distribute themselves evenly through all your train journeys for the year.

It is also worth remembering that uptime guarantees only promise that the hosting service will keep its servers working, so if your site becomes inaccessible to most users during a major product launch because you didn't buy enough bandwidth, you can't expect the hosting service to pay up on its guarantee. Some sites can offer you 100% uptime on selected periods. This can be a good deal, but see everything we have said regarding unlimited bandwidth.

The guarantee is also something you need to discuss with your hosting service. It is worth finding out how much you can expect in terms of compensation for breaches of your uptime guarantee. A small rebate on your next bill is unlikely to be sufficient compensation for losing your site for a week and having all your regular visitors decide to get their news service or whatever elsewhere.

Also remember that hosting services that break their uptime guarantees tend to be poorly run companies, that poorly run companies tend to go bust, and that bankrupt companies are not usually in a position to pay up under compensation agreements. More important than the terms of the guarantee is the *credibility* of the guarantee, which means that you need to ask some more tough questions about how your host intends to meet its commitments. Ask what kind of equipment the hosting service has, and get lots of quotes. If that super-cheap quote for 99.9% uptime comes from a service which appears to have many fewer servers than any of its competitors, it might be too good to be true.

Other services

Hosting companies would be delighted to run all manner of aspects of your site, for a fee, and you may decide to let them provide you with your 'back-end' databases, transaction processing, and so on. It often makes sense to delegate all or most of your technical needs in this way, particularly if neither you nor any of your partners has all that much technical expertise, and buying them from the same company as your hosting will make you a more valuable (and therefore more valued) customer for them. However, you should remember that if your hosting service does the lion's share of the running of your site, its service fee could well account for almost all your profits – assuming, that is, that you make any.

One service you should not delegate and forget is the making of back-ups. The old IT adage is that the only way to learn about taking back-ups is to lose all your data at least once. Don't let this apply to you. Instruct your hosting service to take back-ups of your valuable data – your site, your database and anything else that really matters – at regular intervals (the suitable back-up frequency will depend on the nature of your business, and the speed at which you are gathering data, but taking daily back-ups never killed anyone). Check up on them regularly to make sure that nobody is forgetting to take your back-ups. Ask to see the tapes. It is a chore, but nothing like as much of a chore as rebuilding your whole business from scratch.

Managing outsourced internet services

Nick Hadlow, international computer services manager at SPSS, offers the following advice:

> You need a contract for specialised technical services. The ideal person to manage this (from your side) is someone who's 75% lawyer and 75% [sic] techie. Large companies engaged in technical and engineering projects often have a team of 'contract engineers' who fit this profile. If it wasn't worthwhile using these hybrid creatures, they wouldn't exist.
>
> When negotiating contracts for the provision of IT goods and services always try to insist on having a technician from the vendor present. Salespeople hate it, and will often try to avoid it since the technical specialist is generally willing to engage in a technical discussion which will be more open and factually based than the bland assurances of the salesperson.
>
> Service level agreements (SLAs) are essential, but they need to be properly monitored. Both you and the service provider need to be constantly aware of what your contract entitles you to, and any non-performance should be reported, even if it's trivial. If you let things slide, you will find yourself with a crisis on your hands and everyone shouting at everyone else, when it could have been sorted out two months ago with a friendly email before your three biggest customers got annoyed and went elsewhere.
>
> So, what happens if your service provider doesn't perform? Frankly, you lose. It's unlikely that any guarantee will extend beyond refunding your contract fees for the month in which the service failed, and most providers

won't even go that far. Getting four days' money back for an outage that effectively took you offline for an entire week is poor consolation.

You need full-time access to your servers; you need to be able to apply updates to both content and functionality immediately and securely. Ideally, you would have a technical copy (same OS, same processor, same versions of everything) of the server under your own control so that everything can be tested before uploading to the production environment. In practice, this can be difficult, so you may need to make sure you can properly test and debug your site on the service provider's systems. Some service providers will actually offer you a development and test environment for this, but it will need to be paid for, directly or indirectly.

A second issue with accessing your server is that you want to be able to pull down information from it whenever you want. This is for obvious marketing/commercial reasons, but it also gives you back-ups of the information beyond what is covered by your service provider.

Checklist

Below is a checklist of things you should know before signing a contract with a hosting service. It doesn't cover all the questions a hardcore geek would want to ask, but it gives you enough ammunition not to appear technologically clueless, and to convey the impression that you are someone over whose eyes the wool cannot necessarily be pulled.

Ask these questions of all the companies who are competing for the privilege of hosting your site. Remember that one of the great things about the web is that it is truly worldwide: you can get quotes from hosting services all around the world. But you should probably go with one which is in the same geographical area as you. Even though a service in Western Australia might give the best quote for hosting your page about Croydon, you will want to be able to talk to the support personnel in your own time zone, and to see the service manager face to face from time to time. You also want to pick a service provider in a location where it is convenient for you to come down and look at the back-up tapes.

Bandwidth, including expansion

How much bandwidth will the host allow you, and how does this match up to your needs? If your site takes off more quickly than you expect, will you be able to buy extra bandwidth at a reasonable rate? If they are offering an unlimited bandwidth deal, is it credible?

Uptime

How much uptime are the hosts guaranteeing, and how does this compare to your needs? How credible is it for them to offer this level of uptime? What happens if the uptime guarantee is not met?

Service level

How easy will it be for you to update your site from your own computer? Do you have access to your own 'CGI-bin' directory? The binary common gateway interface directory is the directory where your binary executable programmes (as against HTML files) such as cookies, ordering systems etc. are held. You need this in order for customers to be able to submit orders to your site. Can you use Perl, ASP or other active server pages technology? Will the host take care of your credit card transactions?

Deliverability

How financially secure is the host? What experiences have other customers had with it? Is its technical support good? How onerous is the contract you are about to sign? How easy is it for you to break or renegotiate the contract if your business develops differently? And most importantly, do you trust the people with whom you are considering doing business?

Systems

What software will their servers be running on? Will it be compatible with the software you will use/have used to build your site? Remember the opinions of the industry on Microsoft versus other systems.

Hosting yourself

The alternative to buying in hosting services is to buy the computer and high-bandwidth telecoms connection, and run your own server. This is not for the faint-hearted, but is perfectly possible.

CHAPTER 10
People

Reproduced by the kind permission of BVCA

'Hire people who have done it before, or hire people who have done parts of what you are doing before. It reduces the number of mistakes you make.'

ROB HERSOV, FOUNDER OF SPORTAL

'It's easy to get people to work for you – the problem is finding good people, the right people.'

DOT.COM ENTREPRENEUR

Introduction

Big companies always say their people are their most important asset, but very often they proceed to treat them badly. With small (especially service) companies the cliché is actually true: the people really are the key asset. Your team needs to comprise dedicated people with different skills to offer and a good amount of business experience between them. VCs pay a great deal of attention to the quality of the team you have and the commitment shown by that team, even to the extent, as has been mentioned, of hiring private detectives to check out whether you and your team have exaggerated or even lied about your background and experience.

Who does what

As we have seen (in Legals, chapter 5) the chairman and board of directors have overall responsibility for the direction of the company. The chief executive (or managing director) has responsibility for its day-to-day running. The board are the people ultimately responsible for the company's future, and in particular 'the vision thing', as George Bush once described it. And as Nixon said, 'The buck stops here,' which of course it did. The chairman oversees the company's progress and plays an important part in achieving its strategy by acting as the company's champion with key partners, such as funders, key customers, marketing allies and technology partners. The MD is the person who must make sure that things get done.

It should be the case that everyone called a director is on the board of directors of a company, and there is no one on the board who is not a director. Preferably the IT manager should be made a director so that they can sit on the board, because this encourages the company's technological decisions to be tied in with the company's future strategic direction, although in traditional offline companies the IT manager is often not a director. Ideally there should be someone on the board, preferably the chairman, who has experience of setting up businesses before, preferably net businesses.

In addition, you would ideally have non-executive directors on the board, experienced people with expertise and an independent view to bring to bear on the strategic direction of your company. They would have no responsibility for the day-to-day running of the company.

The essential team

The essential team would comprise the following:

★ chairman;
★ chief executive;
★ IT director;
★ sales and marketing director;
★ finance director.

You need to think very carefully about your team. Venture capitalists and other advisers are putting more and more emphasis on the skills and experience of the team members and less and less on the business idea. Neil Crofts, head of European strategy at Razorfish, finds that 'most groups say they have a team, but what they have is a bunch of titles. When you ask who is going to be responsible for this piece of work, either they say "We all are" or the founder says he will do it all. You need a structured team with proper segments, and that's not usually in evidence.'

The advisers you need

Once your site is active, you will need professional advisers in the fields of:

★ accountancy;
★ law;
★ marketing;
★ technology (probably anyway; you are unlikely to have all the IT skills you need in-house).

Tax and other accountancy issues (such as National Insurance) arise all the time for a trading business, and require an accountant to handle them. It is not merely that you need your everyday tax issues properly dealt with in order not to be breaking the law (see Legals, chapter 5), you will also need an accountancy firm to advise you on the tax consequences of various business decisions, such as the issuing of share options.

Many start-ups develop deeper and more important and useful relationships with their legal and marketing advisors than with their accountancy advisers. If a relationship is to be developed it has to run both ways, meaning commitment and involvement from the company concerned, possibly with a chance to cash in on the upside. This could either be in the form of holding an equity stake (which you may or may not wish to give), or just in the form of having more and more business pushed their way by you as you grow. 'We consider our advisers to be almost like partners in the business' is a common theme of dot.com entrepreneurs, as is 'Our marketing partners have been with us from the start, and they are a real player in our business both in terms of strategic direction and equity holding.'

Notwithstanding the many anti-lawyer jokes that exist in the world, some dot.com start-ups consider their law firms make the kind of contributions to the business you would only expect from partners. But beware: this community spirit is thought by many to be a short-lived phenomenon. They say it arises from the relative newness of e-commerce, which is livening up the professional lives of many a lawyer and marketing consultant by opening up entirely new avenues to explore.

On the other hand, it is rare to find a start-up that regards its outsourced technology suppliers as partners, or one that offers them an equity stake. As Mark Holmes of space2.com explains:

> It was never a real possibility that our webmasters would have an equity stake in the company. That's not to say they weren't interested – they were, especially after the launch. But we didn't want to dilute our equity to people who wouldn't be around for ever, and the reason they won't be with us for ever is because we want to keep working with the leading-edge companies, and they may not be the same as the ones we used at first.

Rather, it is much more common to hear that dot.coms are trying to bring their technology department entirely in-house so that the technology strategy can be more a part of the business strategy, and the difficulty of hiring technology people when you need them may be avoided.

Choosing advisers

The classic way for companies, including net businesses, to choose advisers is to put out the word that they are looking to hire, to ask each firm what it can offer at what cost, and have the answers scrutinised by the most experienced businessperson on your team – usually the chairman. This is called a 'beauty parade'. The first candidates more often than not come to the business through contacts rather than by phoning up relevant companies listed in magazines such as *Revolution* and *New Media Age*, although this route is, of course, possible and sometimes works well.

Your advisers can be large, internationally recognised firms such as Arthur Andersen or Viant, or smaller, possibly more specialised, players. You may find that smaller players are more committed to your project. But when your business goes into 'hyper growth' (the phase of very rapid growth which often follows the first or second round of financing) you might leave a small boutique behind in terms of capacity. 'We wanted agents who could grow with us because we are aiming big' is a common refrain of internet entrepreneurs. You also need to decide whether to go for separate sector specialists in technology, design and strategy or whether to buy a complete package from the integrated internet service companies. Companies such as Razorfish say it can be difficult to integrate advice from several advisers – but you would expect them to use that argument.

A general point on advisers is that many dot.com entrepreneurs, particularly those from the other side of the pond, say that the skill level among European advisers on internet issues is not high. This can often mean that when a company advises you, it is itself going through a learning process. As Sonia Lo from ezoka.com says:

> You should be prepared to really scrutinise the work done by your advisers, and consider whether they have taken longer over the process than they should have done because they too were trying to climb up the learning curve. If you think this is the case, don't just put up with it, but negotiate to pay them less than agreed because of it.

Having said that, many people, such as Guus Keder of transatlantic VC firm Alta Berkeley, observe that the level of internet skills in Europe is rising sharply.

How do you find the people you need?

Your initial, core team should come from people you know or who have been strongly recommended to you. In finding these people you need to spread your net widely and put the word about to all your friends, family and contacts – in a similar way to raising your initial capital. These people have to be really committed to the project because, apart from anything else, if you go to a VC with a team whose members have not already given up their day jobs, you may not be taken seriously.

Your team should reflect the ambitions of your business.

If you are trying to set up a pan-European business, you need to hire people from other countries, or at least people with experience of other European countries. According to Simon Darling, an internet entrepreneur:

> You should begin building a team from day one with the complementary skills and resources to complete the task. I've got very nervous in start-up meetings when a global business is being described and I look around the room to find that everyone sitting around the table is British. Those companies need to get Americans, French, Scandinavians and Germans on to their senior management teams – and fast.

You should also expect to bring on board non-executive directors through the same process. But for subsequent hires you will need to spread the word more widely, and you will probably have to use the services of professional recruiters, of which there are several types.

Organising the recruitment process yourself

In addition to putting the word out to friends, family and contacts that you need people, you should consider advertising job vacancies. There are four areas where you should consider doing this, and you need to use different channels for different people:

★ **Newspapers**. National newspapers are the place to advertise in order to hire new senior members of your team.

- ★ **Trade magazines**. These are the best places to advertise for specialists, such as technology people, and for industry experts.
- ★ **Your own web site**. Always advertise on your own web site if you need people, although you should be circumspect about how many posts you need filled; you don't want to put off either potential customers or potential staff.

Agencies who search: head-hunters

Head-hunters are companies who put out feelers and make phone calls to find people who are willing to be interviewed by them in the first place and potentially be put on to a shortlist for you to interview. This is the most tailor-made way to hire people so it is appropriate only for relatively senior positions. Most head-hunters charge fees upfront for the initial searching process, and again upon generation of a shortlist, and again if you actually hire one of the people on their shortlist. These fees traditionally add up to 33% of the first year's remuneration of the job you are hiring for.

Agencies who select: recruitment consultants and agencies

Recruitment consultants or recruitment agencies are companies that have a database of people appropriate to various different positions on their books, and they send them out to companies on request.

However, they obtain most of their candidates from advertisements they run in various media. These ads do not normally specify which client they are helping, so they often send candidates to more than one client. They charge between 20% and 35% of the first year's salary of the job you are hiring for (depending on the seniority and the scarcity of the candidates), which is payable only if you hire through them.

Fall-off periods

Whatever fee structure you have agreed, most recruitment firms offer you a formal, staggered 'fall-off' period during which they return all or part of their fee if the person you have hired does not stay with your business. But these can vary enormously, so you should consider the scheme you want and negotiate the best deal you can, but usually the proportion of the fee you get back depends on the date the person you hired left your business. One reasonable scheme would be:

★ day one, all money charged returned;
★ between day two and the end of month one, two-thirds of the fee returned;
★ between the beginning of month two and the end of month three, one-third of the fee returned;
★ from month four onwards, no fee returned.

Beware one trick of the trade with fall-offs: most recruiters stipulate that they only honour fall-off periods if their invoice has been paid within their payment period, which is reasonable. It is not reasonable, however, if the payment period is two weeks (or indeed anything less than a month) because most businesses settle invoices on a monthly basis. Be sure to ask whether your agency intends to do this; if it does, try to persuade it either to change its mind or make sure the invoice is settled promptly. Better still, find a different agency.

What to ask your recruiter

You need to test the level of integrity of any agency you use. Here are three good questions:

1. Will the firm always interview any candidates that you meet before sending them to you?
2. Will the firm tell potential candidates where their CVs will be sent? This helps to avoid embarrassing situations when the CV of an apparently loyal employee is inadvertently sent by the agency to the employee's boss's best friend, or even the boss.
3. Once you have hired someone, will the agency refrain from approaching them at a later date to offer them positions in other companies? You don't want your recruiter to poach the same people they found and placed with you.

Employment agencies and job centres

Most employment agencies, such as Manpower, can provide you with staff effectively on a leased basis, which is to say that the staff are employed by the agency rather than you. Such agencies are good resources for hiring temporary staff. Once your business is up and running your demand for clerical and manual staff may greatly increase. Also, although there are other ways of hiring them, there is no harm in posting your vacancies in job centres.

How do you hire the people you need?

The process of hiring people is a difficult one which many start-up entrepreneurs have only experienced from the point of view of the candidate. Taking the other side of the desk, or the other chair in the café, is not necessarily an instinctive process, and it may be one you need to work at. This is not the place for a major treatise on the subject of interviewing, but the following ideas should get you started.

Choosing people

Interviewing is the most commonly used method of hiring people for any job with any firm. In general, however, success at interview is a poor predictor of future success in the job. More rigorous methods exist, such as two-day test centres, psychometric tests and other devices, but few companies have moved away from the traditional interview approach to hiring.

When interviewing, your key task is to look for intelligence, honesty and enthusiasm. Forgetting for the moment the fact that intelligence is hard to define, it is nonetheless the single best predictor of job performance, for almost any job. A very good, although not exclusive, indicator of intelligence is academic record. Another is career track record. But remember that intelligence is not everything. Trustworthiness is vital, as is enthusiasm.

One tip from experienced interviewers is that you should elicit the experience views and opinions of your interviewee before telling them about the experience strategy and direction of you and your company. This is simply, and importantly, in order to prevent you feeding the candidate the lines you want to hear, which they can then just repeat back to you.

Always check references

Stories of people getting jobs they didn't deserve and couldn't do simply by faking their references are legion. It will really make you look and feel very silly if you get caught out by this trick, and your VCs won't be at all impressed when they find out, which they are likely to do. Always follow up your new employees' references.

Attracting people with your package

'The internet is all about human capital.'

ROB HERSOV, FOUNDER OF SPORTAL

What is your package? It is not just the cash, it is also the attractiveness of your business idea or vision to the person you are trying to hire, the personalities of you and the other people in your team, the location of your business and, of course, the cash. The cash comes in three forms: salary, benefits and share options. Of these, the last is the real draw with internet businesses; indeed, many people who join start-ups have to take a pay cut to do so. So get the options right.

Share options are the right to buy shares at a certain date in the future at a price fixed today (normally today's value, or less than today's value). So, for example, you might grant an employee the option to buy 1,000 shares at £1 per share in three years' time. If your shares increase in value because the company has performed well over the next three years to £10 each, the employee then has the right to buy each share for £9 less than its value. This would mean the employee could buy 1,000 shares worth a total of £10,000 for only £1,000.

Obviously you need to assess who needs options to join you and stay with you, and who does not.

When designing your share option scheme, you can choose to use an Inland Revenue-approved scheme or not. Under an approved scheme, the options are exempt from income tax and national insurance if the options are retained for three years. The CSOP (company share option plan) allows options to be granted to any employee up to a market value of £30,000 per employee.

A new EMI (enterprise management incentives) scheme should be available from summer 2000 and will lift the ceiling to £100,000 per employee, but it will be limited to fifteen 'dynamic' executives. Quite apart from the fact that most internet executives feel the £100,000 ceiling is unrealistically low and the three-year vesting period too restrictive, the problem with Inland Revenue schemes is that they take time and bureaucracy to implement. One internet entrepreneur was quoted as saying, 'Each time you go for new rounds of funding your valuation changes, and so does the value of any options granted. We have to get our valuation approved by the Inland Revenue. But do they understand it? It takes them weeks to do anything.'

To avoid the bureaucracy, many internet start-ups opt for unapproved option schemes. Although these schemes can be used for all employees and are unlimited in value, income tax is payable when the options are exercised. In addition, National Insurance is payable on the options when they are exercised. For quoted companies, the implications are significant. They have to make frequent provisions for National Insurance contributions based on the difference between the share price and the exercise price of the options. QXL recently had to put aside £15 million in one quarter to cover potential National Insurance contributions in the context of revenues of just £1.6 million. QXL calls this 'a tax on its share price'.

How many shares for each employee?
by Robert Postlethwaite of capitalstrategies.co.uk

Your starting point is to work out how much benefit you want to deliver to each employee. You may have established that certain employees will be sufficiently satisfied with their share scheme to stay with you if they have the prospect of a multiple of their salary over the next three to five years. That multiple could be anything between five and twenty, depending on their value to the company and the job market for their skills.

For example: assume that your objective is to deliver, through share ownership, a benefit worth £300,000 to a particular employee after five years. Your calculations to determine the number of shares that need to be allocated now depend on your projections for the turnover and profit for your business. Of course, whether this materialises will depend on how successful your business is. If your projections show that the company would grow from a value of £100,000 to £20 million over five years then you should be granting options on about 1.5% of the company's current shares, because if your projections are achieved, a 1.5% holding will grow in value to £300,000. The cost to the employee of exercising the share options will be only £1,500, which is negligible compared to the benefit received.

If you want to grant options phased over several years, the calculation is a little more complicated and would require a spreadsheet to derive the final figures.

How do you keep people?

Because the dot.com revolution is well underway, people interested in joining start-ups who have not already joined one may be hard to find, and people with serious technological internet expertise are seriously in demand. Salaries in this area are going up and up, so once you have someone on board you need to work really hard to try to keep them.

How do you go about doing this? Firstly, ensure they are currently incentivised, revising share option packages if necessary, and also ensure that your company is a great place to work. This means, ideally, that your business should be:

★ successful;
★ prestigious;
★ a fun place to work.

Being interested in the job is usually at least as important to people as the money, so work hard to keep people happy. One way to do this is to manage well.

How to manage

You may not want to manage, you may not have set up your own business in order to become a manager, but you are going to have to learn how to manage well if you are to succeed. Management is about getting things done through people, and one of the first lessons to learn in setting up your business is that you cannot do everything yourself; you need other people to do all sorts of things, so you had better use them effectively. The number of textbooks on how to manage would probably fill a small football field, and this is not the place to summarise them, but here are some of the golden rules of management:

MBO: Manage by objectives

Always be clear about exactly what it is you want to get done. Communicate that message clearly to the person you want to do it, and get agreement on what it is and what would constitute success in terms of an end result. Then judge that outcome only, the end result, not the method by which it was achieved. Some people work in intensive bursts, others work slowly but more or less continuously. The outcome can be the same, although it could appear on the surface that one was more productive than the other.

Involve the people you are directing or managing in the process of planning. This means encouraging people to come up with their own plans of how they are going to achieve the objective and asking them how they think they are doing with the task.

Always ensure that you review progress regularly so that you can forestall problems when they arise, before they become serious. When problems do arise, discuss the issue as soon as you can with the person involved. Do not delay. Remember that annual reviews should bring up no big surprises.

MBWA: Managing by walking around

It's important to be open to your colleagues and staff as much of the time as possible, and not to shut yourself away in an office. This is standard practice at start-ups because there is a great need to pool information.

Adapt the appropriate management style. Your style

'I've learned that my role is less about what I can do and more about what the organisation can do.'

JASON OLIM, CO-FOUNDER OF CDNOW

should vary according to the kind of person you are managing. The following chart may be useful:

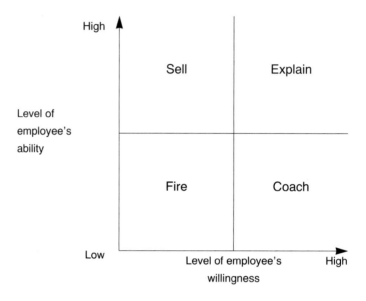

Appendix: Recruiters

Strategy
Douglas Lambias 020 7420 8000
Huntswood 01753 855200
Beament Leslie Thomas 020 7405 3404
IT
Computer People
(computerpeople.com/europe/indexe.htm)
Marketing and PR
The Works (PR) 020 7494 0207
Ball & Hoolahan (classic fmcg marketing) 020 7323 4041
Design
Major Players 020 7836 4041

CHAPTER 11

Launch

'The golden rule is test, test, test. Then have a big party and just go for it.'

DOT.COM ENTREPRENEUR

'If anyone should have been able to launch a site that both arrived on time and works – or at least one of the two – it's boo.com. The company raised £120 million in funding and employs several hundred staff, but it still launched a site that creaks.'

RICHARD LORD, EDITOR, *REVOLUTION*

'Don't hang around, because it is all about speed. If you're not the first to market, you're probably a loser.'

RUPERT LEE-BROWNE, CO-FOUNDER OF EGGSBENEFIT.COM

Soft and hard

Many web companies have a 'soft launch' before their 'hard launch'. The soft launch is when they put up their web site for trials, perhaps inviting a selected number of potential customers to visit and experiment. If necessary, changes can be made before a more formal launch. For example, eBay changed the content, categories and currency options on its UK site after feedback from the soft launch. A soft launch also allows a company to test out fulfilment arrangements (see Growing, chapter 12).

The hard launch is when you hold a big party for as many of the world's press, or trade press, as you can muster, and spend some (just a little) of the VC's money on cheap bulk-purchased champagne. And, crucially, this is when you launch your web site upon an expectant public, and begin the real job of running a business.

When to launch?

Launching your business can mean different things according to how you have handled the feasibility testing period. It may be that this is when you begin your first trades, or it may be that you are now capable of high-volume trades, as in the case of easyshop.com. Alternatively, it may be that you are moving from test customers to real customers, as with businesses such as the car-trading enterprise oneswoop.com.

Judging the timing of a launch is crucial. If you launch too soon, you may not be ready to cope with customers, but if you hold back for too long you may risk losing out to competitors or rivals with the same idea. For example, Kevin Sefton, founder of Y-creds, had originally been developing a web-based loyalty scheme and had signed up two retailers. However, Beenz launched its product first (even though it had only one retailer) and scooped all the publicity. Having lost out to Beenz, Sefton realised he would have to develop a different business. He came up with the idea of Y-creds, an internet bank account for the under-18s (who don't have credit cards).

By the time of the launch you can have achieved a lot of things. For instance, boo.com had a significant brand well before they had launched. (See Marketing, chapter 7.) Of course the company may not live up to the pre-launch promises – that will be up to your collective management and fulfilment ability. Certainly by the time of the launch you *must* have sorted out all aspects of running a business, even if you are intending to start small. So you must have some or all of the following already organised:

★ a team of people with clearly defined roles covering all areas of the business including overall responsibility (chairman and board of directors) and day-to-day running (CEO);
★ business accounts;
★ sales and marketing plans and processes;
★ robust technology;
★ fulfilment processes, which can simply mean provision of content and links if you are providing a service, but if you are to be delivering products it means warehouse facility, warehouse pickers and deliveries (see Growing, chapter 12);
★ customer service arrangements – a help desk, or a call centre dealing with emails, phone calls, letters and faxes (see Growing, chapter 12);

- ★ a solicitor;
- ★ an accountant;
- ★ usable office equipment and office space;
- ★ contingency plans for scaleability (see Growing, chapter 12).

The average time it takes a start-up to go from inception of the idea to the launch of the business is six to nine months. But don't forget the first law of timing: 'Everything always takes longer than you expect.' And the first law of getting businesses up and running, as Sonia Lo, founder of ezoka.com, remarked: 'Everything is difficult.'

Prepare for impact

It's important not to overestimate the impact a launch might make on your business. There are so many web site launches now that it's hard to excite the interest of journalists. Some PR executives think parties are a waste of time and money unless they are part of a well-thought-out promotional strategy: 'You don't get much coverage in return for the sausage rolls and champagne . . . some journalists don't even look at the press pack,' said says Emma Kane of Redleaf Communications, who has worked with several dot.com companies. You need to develop contacts in trade magazines and other relevant organisations in advance of your launch so that you can generate coverage simply by getting on the phone.

In any case, most companies re-launch several versions of their web site within a couple of years, but you really only have an excuse for a party the first time.

CHAPTER 12
Growing

Reproduced by the kind permission of BVCA

'Persistence and perspiration are very, very closely linked. Was it Edison who said genius was 1% inspiration and 99% perspiration? Ideas are easy, but most of what inventing the future is about is execution.'

JEFF BEZOS, AMAZON

'The most vital issue any internet start-up faces is scaleability. Scaling a business up to cope with high volumes, let alone many currencies and languages, is extremely difficult, but absolutely essential.'

MICHAEL ROSS, EASYSHOP.COM

Introduction

The old business adage is that you have to move just to keep standing still; with web businesses it's more like you have to run to keep standing still. What does this mean? It means that in order to keep your competitors at bay you have to develop, grow, expand. This is true whatever business you are in, but it is particularly true if your business relies on technology, as web businesses do, because technology is copiable. Established businesses have to grow in order to keep their shareholders content, and prevent their return on investment falling below that of other companies which could make their shareholders switch. Start-ups face different, but, if anything, more intense pressures.

Start-ups have to grow fast because:

★ For internet businesses, first-mover advantage is very powerful. If you have it, it is vital to try to retain it. The first mover gets all the attention of customers, suppliers, partners and press, and finds itself on a virtuous spiral on which success reinforces success.

★ Any venture capitalists you raise money from to launch your start-up will be taking on a project with considerable risk. Indeed, they may see it as more risky than you do. The understanding on which they undertake this risk (and you receive the money) is that your business will produce significant returns quickly. The only way this is achievable is through a very ambitious growth programme – your VC will be expecting your business to experience hypergrowth.

★ You need to be a market leader or continually to aim to be market leader in order to retain the people you need to keep your business delivering. As we have seen in

People (chapter 10), there will be no shortage of job offers for your people if your company becomes a less attractive place to work, and part of keeping your place to work an attractive one these days is being obviously successful.

You should also grow because you can. Why settle for less than everything?

The timeline of a start-up

But growing quickly is very difficult, and can be exhausting. Crises will certainly occur, different crises in different phases of the business. So far in this book we have discussed the different things you have to do to plan for, set up and run your business: evaluating the idea, writing the plan, doing some research, raising funding, building the technology, etc. Once your business is established it will go through another distinct set of stages, and at each one there are implications for most areas of the business – management, technology, finances, etc.

Now for the crises. Harvard University's Larry Greiner observed that businesses go through a series of crises while growing, as the established business model has to adapt to cope with the changes brought by increases in sales volume and number of employees. The crises are different at each stage and require different solutions.

The usefulness of this model of business growth (see chart) is that you may be able to place your business within it and draw lessons relating to your particular stage of development. Your business will be unique in many ways, but it will also share characteristics with many other businesses in other industries.

The chart below shows the process:

The five stages of business growth

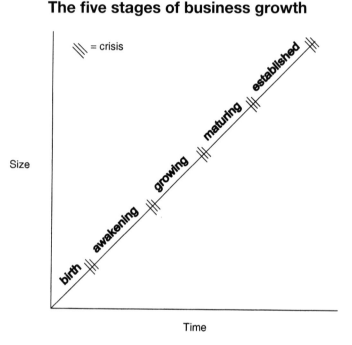

Birth

The first crisis occurs during the initial stages of the business trading. It arises because new staff join the business who do not have the dedication or emotional commitment of the founders. The founders, in turn, are having to deal with transforming an idea into a reality, and can no longer rely on pure adrenalin. The solution is to introduce strong management to drive the business forward. Without this the business can collapse.

Awakening

Under good management, the business evolves into a more formally structured company, which enables employee resources to be channelled more efficiently. In time, however, the employees' knowledge outgrows the systems that have been put in place, and they are then torn between following procedures and taking their own, well-informed initiative. The solution at this stage is strong leadership to re-invent the organisation of the company as a decentralised one and re-motivate the employees.

Growing

With its new decentralised structure, the company introduces bonus schemes (which would be in addition to any share options) to motivate staff, many of whom will generally communicate with top management only non-verbally. In this phase, management considers growing the company by acquisition.

A crisis often occurs as top management becomes concerned at having lost touch with all the disparate parts of the company. A drive to re-centralise can occur, which can lead to management buyouts (MBOs) where a group of managers buys part of the business from the controlling shareholders. This life-stage crisis is resolved by the imposition of formal systems for planning and staff matters.

Maturity

As formal procedures for more and more systems operations are put in place, the company becomes overloaded with red tape and procedures begin to take preference over problem-solving. Innovation is stifled and the company loses ground. This is solved by the adoption of more flexible management approaches and by encouraging team-working.

Established

Of course, there cannot be a final end to this model because all businesses wax and wane. But the peak of development theorised here is a company which is large, but has developed adequately responsive and flexible systems to enable innovation and to flourish despite its size. Stress levels are often high, though, because of the pressure on the company to keep innovating.

Coping with growing: is your business scaleable?

So much for management theory. Internet businesses are also likely to have to deal with various practical challenges as they grow. Some of the most obvious are fulfilment, customer management, partner management, diversification, competitive pressure and internationalisation.

Fulfilment

Perhaps because the web site is such an obviously important part of an internet business, many internet start-ups spend

---

too little time thinking about fulfilment. Some companies only start to address the issue shortly before launch. We heard of a white and brown goods retail site that was still negotiating with logistics companies a week before launch. If you are a retail business, this is far too late. As we saw in Marketing (chapter 7), your ability to deliver goods will be a crucial test of your credibility – if you want to get repeat orders from a customer. You need arrangements that will be robust enough to grow with you.

One of the problems about organising fulfilment is that there are relatively few companies available for this work offering a service at the level of precision and reliability you will want. One of the first places to look is mail-order companies. Sometimes they have spare capacity, and you may be able to find one with some product overlap with what you are offering. Even if there is no product overlap, a mail-order company will have many of the skills in place that you need. They ought to be able to take the information from your web site and process the order and the payment side as well. According to Rob Smeddle of Client Logic, 'There's a massive mystique building up about e-commerce, but it is really just another media for mail order. The engine room for taking orders and sorting out consignments is pretty much the same.'

Another approach is to sub-contract your fulfilment to a small distribution company and hope they can grow with you. There is a risk that they might let you down, but that has not been the experience of many businesses such as lastorders.com, which is distributing beer nationwide.

Although there are variations depending on volumes, mail order costs roughly 10% to 15% of the value of the item (plus post, if appropriate). On a typical order of about £30 a mail-order firm might charge between £3 and £5, depending on the volumes and likely level of returns. Obviously, the

'A lot of people setting up internet businesses are marketing people who spend their time looking at computer screens. They haven't a clue about fulfilment. It's usually the last thing they think about.'

MIKE SHAW-ROBERTS, SURELINE MARKETING

'Fulfilment costs about the same for a Cartier watch as for a £10 radio.'

ROB SMEDDLE, CLIENT LOGIC

'People say that the internet is a global market, but that's a bit frothy. Will you be able to support a global customer?'

RICHARD DOWNS, FOUNDER OF IGLU.COM

percentage cost falls on more expensive items. As with normal mail order, charges are higher for courier delivery.

Customer management

While a basic mail-order level of service may be appropriate for your business in its early days, you may well want to consider outsourcing your customer management as orders and accompanying emails and phone calls swell. Not only do customers expect their emails to be answered within a reasonable time (much faster than traditional mail), but answering emails is time-consuming and may open up continuing dialogue with some customers (which may or may not be a marketing opportunity). Some established internet companies receive vast numbers of emails: eBay in the US receives 50,000 a week. The attractions of outsourcing all this work are obvious. The only snag is the cost.

There are a few specialist firms such as Client Logic that will handle customer management as well as the physical fulfilment of the goods. Adding telephone and email services on to the mail-order package pushes up the cost of the service by about 50% – approaching £7.50 for a typical item. The reasons for this high cost include the following:

★ Many e-commerce sites are generating large numbers of telephone orders.
★ Emails are time-consuming. A typical telephone order takes three minutes; handling a bespoke email takes twelve minutes on average and may lead to further emails. Even with clever software and standardised replies, it's still very time-consuming.
★ Web sites have teething problems. Many crash, leaving

customers uncertain about whether their orders have gone through.

Quite apart from the cost, some companies like Client Logic are often unwilling to price their customer management services on a 'per item' basis. Clients have to choose a certain level of service (one or more people answering the phone, for example) and pay accordingly. The attraction of this approach is that the service can be expanded as the company grows. But start-up companies face an awkward dilemma: risk a poor level of fulfilment or pay a high price for a level of service they might not need. Some US start-ups are trying to get round this problem by attempting to minimise the financial impact of the high price of fulfilment by capitalising it.

Partner management

There is much talk among internet executives about partnerships. It is clear that these can be very valuable relationships, whether in marketing, design, technology or fulfilment. In some cases partnerships may be cemented by some kind of equity ownership, but in other cases the word 'partner' may mean little more than 'we are a very good customer of company X'. The risk for an internet start-up is that you may find that your design 'partner' was suitable for designing your first web site but lacks the experience to develop a much bigger site two years later. You can similarly outgrow marketing and other partners.

Of course, the partner may grow too (or be much bigger in the first place), but these relationships need careful attention. As Richard Downs, co-founder of iglu.com explained, 'Make sure your interests are fully aligned with your partner's. It's a bit like getting married. Even if you haven't thought about divorce, you should be prepared for it. You should at least spend a little time thinking about what your options will be if the partnership breaks up.'

Diversification

As your business grows you may find that your customers ask for things you do not sell. This happens in offline businesses, so expect it to happen online too. You will have to decide whether you can modify your business model without losing control. Obvious examples of diversification include Amazon's move into CDs. It's clear that adding CDs to the supply of books was not a particularly difficult decision, but jungle.com found its customers were asking it to supply CD players as well as CDs. Jungle has now changed its strategy to embrace a range of electronic goods: 'Our whole strategy is now home entertainment.'

The risk for the entrepreneur here is that he or she may be tempted into an un-researched area, or where the returns are much lower than on the business they started. On the other hand, your customers might lead you to a much more attractive market. Retaining an element of flexibility as new opportunities present themselves is one of the biggest challenges to a business that is growing.

Competitive pressure

Another potential challenge for any company is the arrival of new or invigorated competition. If your business is obviously successful, you are likely to attract rivals. There are no rules here, but Simon Darling, an internet entrepeneur, says you have to be able to 'act fast and flexibly when a major threat emerges. Be prepared to rewrite your whole business model to survive.'

Internationalisation

'The internationalisation process has become very short. Traditionally, a company would have expanded after year five. Today it is month six.'

FERDINAND PORAK, DRESDNER KLEINWORT BENSON

Traditionally, a new business would take several years to get firmly established in its country of origin before risking overseas adventures. This makes good business sense, and is good common sense. The business model needs to be tested in practice and possibly modified, and revenue forecasts may prove cautious or optimistic. Sponsorship and partnerships also need to be tested in practice.

However, the global nature of the internet and the potential power of US competitors has changed all that. In the same way that the developmental timetable of internet companies has been compressed from years to months, so the need to internationalise has also been accelerated. The pressure is particularly intense because of the perception that there are many opportunities available in Europe that need to be grasped before US or home-grown rivals emerge.

But taking an internet business overseas can prove almost as difficult as starting again. An internet business which has successfully established itself in one country cannot simply translate the content on the web site for another country and press 'go'. It needs to pay attention to local interests and the differences between countries. For example, silicon.com, a news and recruitment site for the IT industry, has recently raised some £11 million in second-round financing to set up sites in Germany, France and Scandinavia. Silicon is recruiting German IT journalists for its German site and will produce a German site for Germans, even though the underlying idea behind the business is the same as in the UK.

Susan Kish, founder of Zurich's First Tuesday, takes up the theme: 'American businesses treat Britain as just another state and think they can then expand from there into continental Europe. They are learning that there are different regulations, different buying habits, and a need for local distributors.'

Once again, VCs and funders may be able to help with contacts and suggestions. According to Ferdinand Porak of Dresdner Kleinwort Benson (one of the backers of silicon.com), 'Growing internationally requires that a company has the right partners, the right strategic alliances, or it won't be able to succeed. You need someone who can provide you with contacts, expertise, market knowledge and a platform.'

Whether an internet business actually needs to open a physical office in a foreign country will depend on the nature of that business. For example, travel business iglu.com is now setting up web sites in a number of European languages. These do not need to be backed by a physical presence, simply by thorough research into the needs of potential ski customers in other countries.

Quite apart from the challenges of setting up sites in different locations (and some companies seem to set up in a new country each week), the company then has the challenge of managing an international network – a much bigger challenge than a single-office operation in

Clerkenwell. International expansion requires strong financial controls, good communications and frequent travel between offices (and secondments) to allow everyone to share ideas.

Stay healthy

When planning and launching a start-up you generally need to go through months and months of extremely hard work, little sleep and high stress. The bad news is that it is unlikely to get any better for a good while after your business is up and running. The best single way to cope with it is to ensure that you manage other people (and delegate) rather than try to do everything yourself. This obviously means it is important to manage effectively (see People, chapter 10, for tips).

But this won't save you from hard work and tiredness, so you also have to think how best to manage yourself. One problem is that you are very likely to make bad decisions when you are very tired. Ideally, you would therefore avoid becoming very tired, but back here in the real world, the best advice is to look after your health. Here are some tips from dot.com entrepreneurs:

★ 'Try to take half an hour's exercise per day because you are much more able to cope with sleep deprivation if you are fit.'
★ 'Eat well, with good healthy food full of vitamins, whenever possible.'
★ 'Try to cut down on drinking!'
★ 'Don't try to cut down on any established addictions you

have – e.g. don't try to give up smoking or chocolate at the same time you launch your business.'

★ 'When you are very tired and overworked it's easy for someone to catch you off-guard. This is when you are easy prey for all sorts of scam merchants, so beware of Nigerians promising cheques!' (This is a reference to a common scam, primarily conducted by Nigerians, whereby you are asked for your bank details, supposedly in order to deposit a cheque of, for example, £500,000. They claim this is aid money or some such, and that you will receive a commission. In the event, your bank account is, of course, emptied and no cheque is deposited.)

★ 'It helps if you can do the hardest work when you are young!'

> *'Entrepreneurs need to get their own logistics sorted out. Get enough sleep, get a PA and get someone to cook you dinner at home.'*
>
> SUSAN KISH, FOUNDER OF ZURICH'S FIRST TUESDAY

IPO

Introduction

The successful flotations of Freeserve, QXL and lastminute.com and a number of other smaller companies have meant that IPOs (initial public offers) for internet companies have received a huge amount of publicity in the last few months. Public enthusiasm for technology IPOs is reflected in web sites dedicated to information on the subject, including ipo.com for America and epo.com for Europe. Investors have been quick to forget that some stock market debuts, such as that of eXchange holdings, have been less impressive. At the time of writing, eXchange's shares were trading only marginally higher than the price at which they were offered in mid-1999.

For successful companies an IPO can be the moment when founders and funders either realise some of their investments or achieve a market 'valuation' as a reward for all the sleepless nights. The current insatiable public and institutional appetite for internet-related businesses has encouraged many other companies to think they can jump on the same bandwagon. Investment bankers are also queuing up to float internet businesses.

But an IPO may not be an appropriate route for all businesses, and that applies to internet businesses too. In the past, most entrepreneurs would not have dreamt about a stock market flotation when setting up a new business. It would certainly not have been a central part of the plan. In the past, there were considerable regulatory obstacles and overwhelming lack of interest on the part of investors for risky start-ups and loss-making businesses.

An IPO is not the only way to achieve a stock market quotation: there are introductions and placings too (see below). Nor is a stock market flotation the only way to realise the partial or complete value of your business. In fact, many funders are wary of entrepreneurs who appear set on the idea of an IPO. This is because by the time the business is ready for flotation, the founder is likely to be a minority (albeit significant) shareholder. The various funders and backers will probably own a majority of the shares, and they may judge that a trade sale or a sale to a partner or competitor might yield more value than an IPO. These transactions receive far less publicity and press coverage than IPOs, but are a far more frequent exit route for VCs.

Nevertheless, the spectacular success of internet-related companies has changed the picture to some extent: the London Stock Exchange has relaxed its rules to make it easier for companies with shorter trading histories to join the market. Freeserve was floated on the main market in mid-1999 only nine months after being set up. There are also concrete reasons why an IPO or another form of flotation is useful for a company.

Flotation

A stock market quotation should:

★ provide access to capital for growth – both at the time of flotation and later;
★ create a liquid market for shares, bringing in new investors and allowing existing shareholders to sell;
★ facilitate acquisitions by providing a currency – quoted shares;
★ raise the company's public profile;

* enhance the company's position with customers and suppliers;
* motivate employees through share schemes;
* improve efficiency, because of improved systems and controls;
* place a value on the business.

Against these considerable benefits, companies have to weigh the drawbacks and considerable costs:

* **Management time**. Preparing for flotation will absorb a huge amount of time – much more than managers usually expect. There will be a lot of work for about six months before flotation, and the work will be pretty much full time in the three months prior to listing. This will distract you from running the business. Is your business robust enough to survive such distraction?
* **Cost**. Flotation is an expensive business, even on the AIM. A flotation on the main market usually costs at least £500,000, and a big IPO with a roadshow will cost several times that. These costs are mostly the fees for advisers, and different advisers are paid different amounts and in different ways. Accountants and management consultants may be paid according to the time spent, or you may negotiate fixed fees. Lawyers rarely accept fixed fees. Brokers are generally paid a proportion of the money raised. For a small company, the costs of flotation may represent a significant chunk of the cash being raised. For example, freecom.net's flotation costs were £630,000, to raise £12.5 million. For larger flotations, although the costs get larger (the Freeserve float cost £9.3 million), the figure is usually a smaller percentage of the capital raised.
* **Disclosure**. Flotation involves writing a prospectus for

potential new investors. This will also 'disclose' your business plan to anyone else who wants to read it. You also have to discuss your prospects (in a circumspect way) and show detailed historical financial figures for the business. After flotation, companies have to report results on a much more frequent basis and more publicly than private companies.

★ **Loss of privacy**. A public company cannot be run on a 'lifestyle' basis. If you have been happy to blur the financial distinction between your private life and your company, that has to end. Public companies have to disclose directors' salaries, and there are also considerable restrictions on directors' share dealings, etc.

★ **Loss of control**. Although by this stage entrepreneurs are used to the idea of swapping equity for cash, a flotation takes that process further. Substantial acquisitions have to be approved by shareholders, and if the company performs badly it can be taken over, depending on the proportion of equity remaining in the directors' hands.

★ **Exposure to market conditions**. Market trading conditions, which are completely outside the control of management and which may bear little relation to the 'real economy', may affect the valuation of the company. In extreme conditions, for instance, this can force the cancellation or postponement of a flotation – but not of the fees incurred up to that point!

> *'Thrusting a start-up into the public arena on day one is not a good thing to do . . . we did not grasp control in the way we should have done.'*
>
> STEPHEN MURPHY,
> VIRGIN FINANCE
> DIRECTOR

Regulatory hurdles

There are also regulatory obstacles to be overcome. These are detailed in the Stock Exchange's Yellow Book. The main hurdles are:

- ★ **Audited trading record**. Companies have to have a three-year trading record with audited accounts. (This condition has been relaxed for certain technology companies – see below.)
- ★ **Independence**. The company must be able to demonstrate that it can carry on its business independently from the influence of any major shareholder (over 30%).
- ★ **Shares in public hands**. Once floated, at least 25% of the shares have to be in public hands (but see below).
- ★ **Market capitalisation**. Must be over £700,000, which is not usually a problem.
- ★ **Incorporation**. Companies normally have to be a public limited company (PLC).
- ★ **Directors**. They have to attest that they do not have conflicts of interest (for example with partners, suppliers or customers) that might be prejudicial to the interests of outside shareholders.

For technology companies some of these hurdles have been lowered. For example, the Stock Exchange has waived the three-year trading requirement. But in return, companies have to report trading on a quarterly basis (rather than every six months), and they also have to come to the market with a capitalisation of more than £50 million, and at least £20 million worth of shares must be on offer to investors.

AIM is an alternative

Technology and other companies can also consider joining the AIM (alternative investment market), set up to trade shares of small companies where several of the listing regulations, including those on minimum share offering, acquisitions and tax, are less onerous than on the main market, particularly in terms of the trading record. There is no minimum requirement, but if the record is shorter than two years, directors owning more than 1% of the shares have to agree to hold on to those shares for at least a year after flotation.

There are several other advantages of joining the AIM rather than the main market. It is cheaper, for a start, usually costing between £250,000 and £300,000. Some companies joining the AIM keep costs down by choosing a 'placing', offering shares to a limited group of shareholders, or an 'introduction' where no new money is raised. In both these instances marketing costs are much reduced, but the publicity the company receives is also much lower.

But then some companies find they get more coverage than on the main market, where smaller companies often get ignored. According to Dru Edmonstone at Durlacher, an investment bank, 'By and large AIM companies receive more financial press coverage than their equivalent-sized companies on the main market, thus increasing their potential exposure.'

One way to assess the suitability of AIM for your company is to observe the companies coming to that market. Since the start of 1999 there has been a sharp rise in internet-related companies arriving on AIM. About half the companies have been investment vehicles, companies raising cash to invest in internet start-ups (see Funding, chapter 6). But there has also been a strong crop of actual internet-related businesses:

★ Affinity Internet
★ Channelfly.com
★ Freecom.net
★ Gaming Internet

- ★ Gameplay.com
- ★ Globalnet Financial.com
- ★ Harrier Group
- ★ Infobank International
- ★ Internetaction.com
- ★ Online Classics
- ★ Oneview.net
- ★ Print Potato.com
- ★ Rex Online
- ★ RTS Networks
- ★ Sports Internet Group
- ★ Totally
- ★ Virtual Internet.net

You can often download a flotation prospectus from a company's web site. You can then see the amount of work that goes into a full prospectus and whether it is appropriate for your company to be thinking in those terms.

Although requirements for the AIM are more relaxed than for the main market, companies do have to retain a nominated adviser (a 'nomad'). If the broker resigns for any reason and the company cannot find a replacement within a month, the company's quote on AIM is cancelled.

TechMARK

A listing on AIM can be a stepping stone towards the London Stock Exchange's new group of technology companies, known as techMARK. This is a group of nearly 200 companies quoted on the main market ranging from the very small to Vodafone. The companies that have joined the main market with shorter-than-normal trading records go into this group.

Ofex

Outside the Stock Exchange's markets, companies can also have their shares traded on Ofex, a matched bargain market. There are about 200 companies currently quoted on Ofex. At the time of writing Ofex had been used by some 12 internet companies to raise funds. Examples include Nettec, Asian Onlinean and sportingbet.com. Companies thinking of applying need a registered adviser such as an accountant or a lawyer, and should probably attend one of Ofex's seminars to get to know more about the trading arrangements.

EASDAQ and NASDAQ

Other listing options for technology companies include EASDAQ, the European technology market based in Brussels. This was launched in 1995 in response to the success of NASDAQ, the US high technology exchange. EASDAQ now has about 70 companies quoted, but it has yet to match the popularity of its US rival.

A small number of European companies choose to have their main quote on NASDAQ. For example, Quadstone, a Scottish software company which designs software to monitor internet customer behaviour, plans to list its shares on NASDAQ in late 2000. A significant number of companies choose to be listed in several markets at once. For example, Freeserve is listed on the stock exchange in London and on NASDAQ.

What investors look for

Whether a company chooses to list on the main market or AIM, it still has to convince investors that they should invest in it. Not all IPOs are a success; some flop because investors are not convinced about the prospects for the business.

The process of courting investors for an IPO is similar to the process of raising funding earlier in the life of the company. That is not surprising, because you are asking people to do the same thing: swap cash for equity. The difference with an IPO is that you will have a team of advisers who have often gone through the process several times in the past and who will help you sell your business. But whatever the quality of your advisers, you will still need to convince investors that you have:

★ **A viable business plan**. The plan forms a major part of the prospectus and it will also include all the historical financial information on your company and the assumptions about the future development of your business. You will need to show how you will spend any fresh capital you are raising.

★ **Good management**. Like VCs, institutional investors look at the experience and credibility of management. Frequent changes don't look good, and they like to see outside experience at the non-executive director level.

★ **Track record**. Usually investors prefer companies with a solid track record. In the case of technology companies, where this requirement has been relaxed, investors look even more carefully at revenue patterns and future assumptions.

★ **An acceptable valuation**. Investors compare companies preparing to float with others already quoted.

Normally, investors are unwilling to pay a premium unless there are very special circumstances.

★ **An acceptable shareholding structure**. An IPO is rarely the moment when the founder cashes in their chips and heads instantly for their yacht. Investors are usually suspicious if management plans to sell too great a part of their stake and usually prefer them to retain a substantial stake, for at least six months.

The process

If flotation sounds complicated and time-consuming, it is. The London Stock Exchange publishes a useful introduction to the process from the company's point of view. It includes an outline timetable and further information about the issues a company has to address before it embarks on the IPO route.

If you do believe your company is in the correct position to go for an IPO you have to make sure the other owners of the business – VCs and other backers – agree. If they believe a trade sale is a more realistic route, then you may well have to fall in with them. You cannot mount an IPO without the backing of the owners of the business. Some VCs are quite happy to start the process of an IPO simply to bring potential trade buyers out into the open.

You also have to make sure the management team is in complete agreement about moving from a private company to a quoted company. Stockbrokers say that disagreements often come out late in the process, and they can be very damaging.

Picking advisers

Once you have agreed with the other owners and managers of the business that an IPO is the best option, you need to appoint advisers. In the first instance you need a sponsor (from the list of sponsors approved by the Stock Exchange). You may also need a corporate broker if it is a big issue. You will need a legal firm that can handle the huge task of verifying the whole prospectus and preparing other documents associated with the listing. You may be able to use your existing firm of accountants, but they will need to be familiar with the requirements of flotation. You may also want to appoint public relations advisers.

Most companies organise a beauty parade of sponsors. A sponsor will usually put on a short presentation and you can then ask them informally about their knowledge of the sector, the kind of valuation they might expect for your company, and whether they have access to an appropriate investor base. It is worth bearing in mind that sponsors will also be assessing whether you would be an attractive company to sponsor. It helps if you have done some research about valuation so you can discuss this issue at the outset.

One way of identifying possible sponsors is to see who is helping other companies in your sector. You may or may not be better off with a big investment bank. You need to make sure your flotation will be handled by an experienced director and that the person you meet at the beauty parade will not be replaced by someone less experienced.

What next?

As we have noted, flotation is unlikely to be the moment an entrepreneur buys that Picasso they had their eye on. There are usually lock-ins specifying the minimum period leading executives have to stay with a business. Nevertheless, flotation does establish a market valuation (albeit volatile) for a founder's stake, and this may encourage him or her to consider future options.

Assuming the business continues to develop, at some stage the entrepreneur should be able to cash in. At that stage, the entrepreneur has three options:

★ Build up the quoted company further by way of organic growth and acquisition.
★ Step back from day-to-day involvement and become involved in other ventures. Some become serial entrepreneurs. Look at the examples of Chris Evans in the biotechnology industry or Giles Clarke, who set up Majestic, then Petsmart, and is now bringing StepStone to the market. Other entrepreneurs prefer to use the experience (and/or cash) they gained establishing one company to advise and invest in other ventures. Tim Jackson helped found QXL and is now working with a $500 million European fund at venture capitalist Carlyle Internet Partners. Hermann Hauser founded Acorn computers, and now runs the Amadeus venture capital fund.
★ Spend more time at the golf club.

Appendix

The London Stock Exchange: londonstockex.co.uk (020 7797 1000) – publishes a *Practical Guide to Listing* which looks at the pros and cons of a stock market listing from a company's point of view. It also publishes information about

AIM and techMARK, as well as details of approved sponsors.

★ AIM information unit 020 7797 4404
★ Ofex: ofex.co.uk (020 7488 3334)
★ EASDAQ: easdaq.com (020 7786 6400 or 0032 2 227 6520)

AIM advisers and brokers

Teather & Greenwood
Brewer Dolphin
Beeson Gregory
Charles Stanley
Collins Stewart
Seymour Pierce
Peel, Hunt
Grant Thornton
West LB Panmure
John East
Investec Henderson Crosthwaite
Brown Shipley
Sutherlands
Insinger Townsley
Durlacher

CHAPTER 14
Outro

TIMELINE

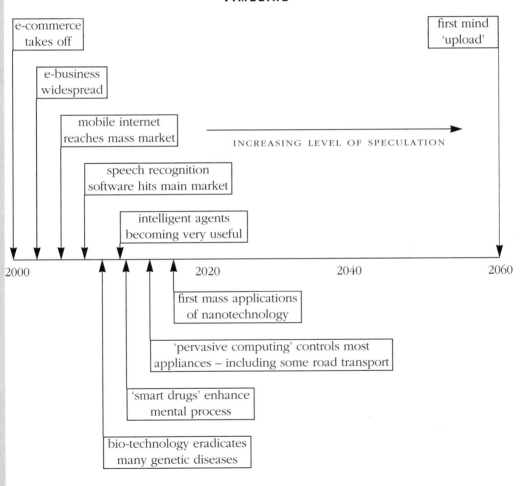

What does the future hold?

A consistent theme of commentary about life in the internet age is that it is faster: a year in the offline world is several years in the internet world.

So what happens next? Is the internet a one-off step change for humankind, or is it simply part of the continuous acceleration of daily life? Will the pace of change in our lives continue to increase?

Many people thinking about this issue believe that the pace of change is set to continue accelerating. Bill Gates's comment on the matter is: 'You ain't seen nothin' yet!' So what does the future hold?

Already e-commerce is giving way to e-business, as traditional offline businesses move to make themselves web-enabled, integrating the internet into every aspect of their work, using the web to communicate with suppliers, employees and other stakeholders as well as customers.

The next wave seems likely to be WAP – wireless application protocol. Beyond that we can look forward to 'pervasive computing', where microprocessors are embedded in every material thing around us: in our clothes and our spectacles as well as our cars.

Attention may then turn away from computers for a while, as we become caught up in the flurry of developments thrown up by biotechnology. This area of science will soon give us a multitude of complex and difficult questions to answer, and dilemmas to resolve. Pharmaceutical firms and biotechnology firms are making it possible safely to enhance the intelligence of our children, eradicate most genetic diseases, and perform a host of other remarkable feats.

But these benefits will raise awkward ethical and social

questions, and the technologies will, at least initially, be expensive. How will we determine who has access to them? How will we decide who gets to make their kids smarter, stronger, better-looking? Will we try to ban the whole process? Will we be *able* to ban it?

Looking yet further ahead, there are many fascinating possibilities, such as nanotechnology, the production of tiny robots which assemble physical objects to order, starting at the atomic level and working up.

But perhaps the most extraordinary notions of what the future may hold take us back to computing. This final chapter looks at some of the astonishing ideas which have been put forward about what will happen later this century if the pace of change in computing science keeps increasing.

These ideas seem like science fiction today, but who knows? They may be completely wrong, but they just may be right. They include the notion that we are not very far away from a total transformation in the nature of humanity. They suggest that we are on the threshold of the creation of a whole new species. Oh yes – and that you might become immortal. Warning: if you don't like strange ideas, stop reading now!

Moore's Law

What is driving the pace of change today is the dramatic increase in computer processing power, and the increasing sophistication in how we use it. Change is being driven by technology.

In the mid-1960s, Gordon Moore, one of the founders of Intel, observed that the processing power of computers is doubling every eighteen months or so. This observation became known as Moore's Law.

If you double something repeatedly you get an exponential curve. One of the features of an exponential curve is that whatever stage of the process you look at, it always seems that the past has been almost flat and the present almost vertical. Thus, from our perspective at the start of the twenty-first century it looks like the increase in processing power was incredibly slow and painful in the first few years, and has been very fast in the last couple of years.

The interesting thing is that if Moore's Law holds true into the future, the curve is going to look exactly the same in ten years. And in twenty years. In 2020, people will look back and think that late twentieth-century computers were improving very slowly compared with the pace of change they are seeing.

There may be nothing inevitable about Moore's Law, of course, but it has been a reliable predictor of progress so far, and computer scientists believe it will continue to hold true for years to come.

Admittedly, the history of technology is full of people making wildly inaccurate projections by extrapolating past trends, i.e. assuming the future will be like the past. In the nineteenth century Thomas Malthus predicted imminent disaster due to over-population; in the 1970s many people were afraid that the world economy would grind to a halt within a few years as reserves of oil were exhausted.

But history also holds plenty of examples of people making what seem in retrospect to be absurdly conservative forecasts about the growth of technology. Alexander Graham Bell, the inventor of the telephone, worried that he was being boastful when he speculated publicly that one day there might be a telephone in every single city in the USA! One of the early bosses of IBM estimated the world market for computers at a grand total of five machines!

Will the exponential power of computing tail off, or stop? Of course it might, but there are good reasons to think that it won't. The improvement of the silicon chip we use today is set to reach its physical limits around 2020, but already a number of replacement technologies are being developed, including three-dimensional chips, optical computing, DNA computing, nanotubes and, ultimately, quantum computing. There is no room to go into the details here, but many computer scientists believe that Moore's Law has many years left in it yet.

What will happen to computers if Moore's Law holds?

Binary computers are only about 60 years old. The first working one was built to crack the German forces' Enigma code during the Second World War. Computers have come a long way since Enigma. A reasonable desktop computer today has roughly the same processing power as an insect. It cannot do what an insect can do, because its software has not been designed to. Then again, a wasp cannot run Doom 2.

If Moore's Law does hold, in about twenty-five years' time a desktop computer should have the same processing power as a human brain. What does that mean?

A human brain contains around 100 billion neurons, each with around 1,000 connections to other neurons. This gives a total of 100,000 billion connections, each capable of

200 calculations per second, so the brain is capable of 20 million billion calculations per second. A component performing 200 calculations per second may sound fast, but in computing terms it is actually rather slow. The brain is a massive but slow parallel processor. Thus, we are very good at things which require massive parallel processing, such as recognising faces. We are not so good at things which require lots of sequential thinking, such as arithmetic.

At the moment, a personal computer selling in the US for $1,000 can manage 600 million calculations per second. Doubling this every eighteen months, applying Moore's Law, means that by 2034, the equivalent machine will be able to execute 30 million billion calculations per second – more than a single human brain. Supercomputers will probably equal the processing power of a human brain a few years earlier.

And what if the exponential curve keeps on working? Thirty years later, in 2064, a PC would have the same power as a million human brains, and in 2079 it would have the same as a billion human brains. Some time at the end of this century a single PC would have the same computing power as the entire human race combined. That is an amazing prospect.

Will powerful computers be conscious?

Many people think that the consciousness we experience is simply a subjective manifestation of the electrochemical processes going on in the brain. They argue further that consciousness in general is a by-product of sufficiently complex and powerful information processing. They conclude that if and when computers become as powerful as the human brain, they will also become conscious.

Many people reject this idea. Some do so on religious grounds: they see the conscious mind as intimately linked to the soul, and the soul as not capable of reduction to purely physical phenomena. Others argue that consciousness springs from the particular way our brains are configured, or the particular material they are made of, and that computers would have to mimic this configuration or substance in order to become conscious.

We probably will not know who is right unless and until somebody creates a true artificial intelligence. But it seems at least a possibility that we will have a situation within a generation where computers are intelligent and conscious, and think a great deal faster than us – and continuing to get smarter than us at an exponential rate.

Would this be the 'Skynet scenario' from the *Terminator* movies? Could we be creating an evolutionary competitor which will destroy us? Not necessarily.

Merging with the machines

Some people argue that the way to avoid being superseded as a species will be to link our brains directly to smart computers, to 'upload' our minds into computers.

Is this feasible? We have learned enormous amounts about how the brain works in the last 20 years thanks to sophisticated scanning techniques such as magnetic resonance imaging and optical imaging. But there is still an enormous amount to be done. To upload a mind may entail mapping every neuron in its brain, and determining how they all interact with each other.

But, if the computing power available to us continues to

increase exponentially, the growth of our understanding of the brain will accelerate. Unless you adopt the view that there is something magical, spiritual, and in principle unknowable about the brain, we may well be able to create a new home for a person's mind inside a computer.

In short, we could be on the threshold of the time when mankind will create a new species. Intelligent machines will become a new species, and we will merge with them. The traditional term for beings which are part-human, part-machine is cyborgs, but that sounds rather sinister. A better title would be 'transhumans'.

Three things about being transhuman

Transhumans will not be dependent on their bodies for survival. This has two major implications.

Firstly, transhumans should be immortal. They would 'back up' their minds continually so that if they were run over crossing the street their minds and their memories could be recovered. And in the unlikely event that computers are still prone to crashing late in this century, the back-up would prevent that being fatal. (This does raise some interesting questions about the nature of personal identity, but there is no space for that debate here.)

Secondly, transhumans could inhabit many different bodies during their long lives, bodies which would have major improvements on human flesh and bone. They would not get old or wrinkled, they would not need to experience pain, and they could have senses enormously more acute than the ones we have now.

A third aspect of transhuman life is that the new species would have permanent and immediate access to all the knowledge there is. No more tortuous hours and days spent learning languages or sciences: they would just download any information they need in a fraction of a second.

The dangerous transition

The creation of transhumans may sound too good to be true, and the idea that it could start to happen during the lifetimes of people alive today is surely astounding. And of course it may not happen. Moore's Law might fail, or it might turn out that consciousness does not arise, and cannot be sustained.

But even if transhumans do step out of science fiction and into reality, the transition may be far from easy. There is likely to be great social trauma if and when a critical mass of people realise that technology is about to make *Homo sapiens* obsolete. Religious organisations in particular could have a hard time accepting the situation. There may be riots, revolutions, wars, even complete global social breakdown. Maybe it is time people started thinking seriously about these questions.

Ray Kurzweil has explored many of these ideas more fully in his book *The Age of Spiritual Machines*. Interestingly, the paperback version bears an endorsement by Bill Gates. Like the man said, 'You ain't seen nothin' yet!'

Glossary

Ad click rate

The percentage of ad views resulting in an ad click, sometimes referred to as the 'click-through rate' or 'click rate'.

Ad clicks

The number of times users click on an ad banner.

Ad pages sold

The number of page views an internet company sells to advertisers. The percentage of the total available page views that are sold is referred to as the 'sell-through rate'.

ADSL

Asymmetric digital subscriber line, a digital transmission technology that allows very fast connection to the internet. It is described as asymmetric because the user is able to receive more data than they can send in a given period.

Ad views

The number of times an ad banner is downloaded and (presumably) seen by visitors. This statistic usually understates the number of actual ad impressions because of caching by browsers. This statistic corresponds to 'net impressions' in traditional media.

B2B (business to business) commerce

Transactions between companies and organisations.

B2C (business to consumer) commerce

Transactions between companies/organisations and individual consumers.

Backbone

A high-speed line that forms a route within a network. The size of a backbone is relative to the size of the network it serves.

Bandwidth

Bandwidth is a measure of information transfer, and it is the quantity by which web hosting services are usually priced. Bandwidth is measured in megabytes (1,000 bits) per unit of time, usually seconds. A full page of text is about 16,000 bits. A fast modem can carry about 56,000 bits in one second. Video usually requires about 10,000,000 bits per second.

Banner

An advertisement on a web page that is normally 'hot-linked' to the advertiser's site.

Browser

A browser is an individual user's interface with the World Wide Web. The browser follows hypertext links and allows you to move from one web site to another.

Browser caching

Browsers store recently used pages on a user's disk to speed up access if the site is revisited. The browser then displays pages from the disk instead of requesting them from the server. As a result, servers routinely under-count the number of times a page is viewed.

Cache

A temporary storage for frequently or recently accessed data. The CPU holds an internal cache while an external cache is on the motherboard of a computer.

Churn rate

This is the proportion of subscribers or users leaving a service in a given time period.

Ciphertext

Encrypted text.

Click-through rate

The proportion of viewers of a web page that click on, or choose to view, a banner advertisement. For example, if five viewers click on an ad out of every hundred page views, the click-through rate is 5%.

Community

A group of people who regularly visit a web site in order to take part in some form of group activity around a common interest, which could be anything from computer games to beekeeping. The community web site may include competitions, discussions, news and links to other sites relevant to site visitors.

Cookie

A small file on which a web server holds information about an individual user of a web page.

CPM

CPM is the cost per thousand for a particular web site. A web site that charges £10,000 per banner and guarantees 500,000 impressions has a CPM of £20 (i.e. 10,000 divided by 500).

CSP

Commercial service provider. A business that focuses on support for e-commerce and e-business operations.

Domain

The unique name of an internet site; for example www.amr.co.uk. In the US there are six widely used domains: .com (commercial), .edu (educational), .net (network operations), .gov (US government), .mil (US military) and .org (organisation). Other, two-letter, domains represent countries: .uk for the United Kingdom, etc. It is likely that .eu will be introduced in Europe.

DVD

Digital versatile disk, a high-density compact disc that allows the storage of large amounts of data.

E-business

Making the whole of an organisation or business transparent online so that all interested parties can transact with it; not just customers, but also suppliers, employees, investors, government bodies, environmentalists, etc.

E-commerce

The use of electronic methods (usually the internet) to carry out transactions rather than paper and mail. However, the term e-commerce is often used with particular reference to the internet.

EDI (electronic data interchange)

A process by which companies can send structured business documents to their suppliers and customers using computers and telecommunication lines instead of paper, fax machines and mail. EDI allows companies to exchange documents from computer to computer without human intervention, thereby removing the need to re-key transaction data into internal systems on both sides of the transaction. The process is widely used in the automotive industry, for instance.

EDI documents

Standardised electronic business documents, such as purchase orders, invoices and advanced shipping notices, that can be sent from computer to computer without human intervention (see EDI).

Extranet

When a company opens its internal network to selected suppliers or customesr, this intranet becomes an 'extranet'. Authorised users can then view the information on the intranet.

Firewall

A barrier between a corporate network and the internet that is supposed to keep the corporate network secure from hackers and only allows access to authorised corporate users.

FTP

File transfer protocol is one of the most basic ways of transferring information over the internet.

Hacker

A programmer who breaks into computer systems for fun, or to expose security lapses.

HDSL

High-speed digital subscriber line, a transmission technology also known as repeaterless T-1. HDSL provides transmission speeds of 1.544 Mbps up to 12,000 feet compared with T-1, which can only transmit up to 4,000 feet before repeaters are necessary. Like ADSL, HDSL also uses existing copper cabling.

Hit

In the context of the World Wide Web, a 'hit' means a single request from a web browser for a single item from a web server. The server will count four 'hits' if a web browser displays a page containing three graphics: one 'hit' for the HTML page and one for each of the three graphics. Hits are often used as a very rough measure of load on a server – for example, 'a million hits a month'. However, because each hit can represent anything from a request for a small document to a complex search request, the actual load on a machine from any one hit is almost impossible to calculate.

Host

A company providing servers and computers that run web sites for other organisations.

HTML

Hypertext markup language is a code used to make hypertext documents for use on the web. HTML is used around blocks of text to show how they should appear. HTML allows text to be 'linked' to another page on the internet.

HTTP

Hypertext transfer protocol allows the transfer of hypertext and hyperlinked data on the web.

Hypermedia

Pictures, videos or audio on a web page that link to other pages.

Hypertext

Text that can be chosen by a reader (normally by clicking) and which causes another document to be retrieved and displayed.

Impression

The viewing of a web ad by a web user. For the advertiser, one page view equals one impression.

Incubator

An organisation which nurtures embryonic internet business ideas.

Internet

The internet is a global network of computers, itself made up of smaller computer networks, variously connected to the world's telecommunications infrastructure. Data is exchanged using internet protocols.

Internet commerce

A subsector of electronic commerce in which goods and services are bought or sold using the World Wide Web as a communications medium. Companies that want to conduct internet commerce create web sites that function as virtual stores through which customers can access product information, place orders and make payments. Some companies only use the web, and some companies use the web combined with traditional outlets.

Intranet

Many companies have built in-house networks using the same software standards as the internet. Companies use intranets to distribute information and data around their offices. Intranet activities usually take place behind secure 'firewalls' to prevent unauthorised access.

IP address

Every system connected to the internet has a unique internet protocol address, which consists of a number in the format A.B.C.D where each of the four sections is a decimal number from 0 to 255. Most people use domain names instead, and the resolution between domain names and IP addresses is handled by the network and the domain name servers.

ISDN

The integrated services digital network moves up to 128,000 bits per second over a normal phone line at almost the same cost as a normal phone call.

ISP

Internet service providers are companies that provide telephone network access to the internet to businesses and consumers.

JAVA

Programming language from Sun Microsystems that allows web users to access pages and to click on symbols or words.

M-commerce

Transactions through mobile phones.

Metatags

Metatags are words in the HTML code of a web site which search engines look at when compiling their list of sites relevant to someone's search. Metatags should be words that are directly relevant to your site.

Page views

The number of pages of a web site seen by customers in a given period. Page views may overstate ad impressions if users choose to turn off graphics (often done to speed browsing). Page views are also referred to as page impressions.

Portal

A web site which is a first port of call for visitors and offers access to a large number of other web sites as well as providing its own content. Some of the biggest portals are built around search engines such as Yahoo!, Excite and Alta Vista. Portals tend to attract large numbers of visitors through a large breadth of information and services – email, TV listings, travel services and share prices – but may lack the depth of content to retain visitors.

Protocol

A standard specification for how computers communicate with each other.

Scaleable

A term for an internet business model that can be scaled up for very fast growth.

Search engine

A search engine offers users the ability to search web sites for specific words or phrases. The information is then indexed in a database to allow immediate retrieval of relevant sites.

Sell-through rate

The percentage of available page views sold to internet advertisers in a given period.

Server

A computer connected to the internet and used to host web sites.

SME

Small or medium-sized enterprise, usually meaning between 10 and 250 employees.

T-1

A high-speed (1.54 megabits/second) network connection.

T-3

An even higher-speed (45 megabits/second) internet connection.

TCP

Transmission control protocol helps to ensure that information travels safely on the internet.

Unique users

The number of different individuals who visit a site within a specific time period. To identify unique users, web sites rely on some form of user registration or identification system (see cookie).

URL

A universal resource locator is the address of an item (page, graphic, database field) on the web (for example, www.amr.co.uk).

Vortal

A vertically integrated portal is a web site that contains a large amount of content and services of interest to a particular online community, and which is therefore an end destination.

WAP

Wireless Application Protocol, one of the technologies enabling internet access through mobile phones.

Website

A location on the web belonging to a company or individual containing information in the form of text, graphics, sound, video and software. Some sites merely provide information; others are interactive and have features that prompt visitors to remain for longer periods. Still others are e-commerce sites, which enable visitors to buy products or services online.

Net jargon

★ **Bitlegging** (cf bootlegging) – theft of intellectual property online.

★ **Bricks and mortar** – offline business.

★ **Business angels** – wealthy people who invest in business start-ups.

★ **Business archangels** – <u>very</u> wealthy people, like Paul Allen or Bernard Arnault, who invest in business start-ups.

★ **Clickocracy** – a system in which consumers rule because of price transparency.

★ **Clicks and mortar** – combination of e-commerce and traditional business.

★ **Cracker** – a hacker who wants to steal or destroy information.

★ **Cyber-squatter** – someone who buys a domain name in cyberspace in the hope of selling it later for profit.

★ **Digerati** – the digital elite.

★ **Ditcherati,** Shoreditch digerati – see digerati.

★ **Doorbell-ware** – a web site containing nothing more than contact details.

★ **Dot bomb** – an unwise dot.com investment.

★ **Dot hon** – a well-connected dot.com executive.

★ **Elevator pitch** – a speech lasting no longer than an elevator ride which is designed to explain to potential investors why they should back your idea.

★ **E-vangelist** – person who is obsessed with the internet and thinks it is a force for ultimate good.

★ **Hortal** – horizontal portal that cuts across several sectors.

★ **Intellectual bandwidth** – a person's available time.

★ **Knowbie** – someone who can help a newbie.

★ **Macwater** — (technological backwater) critical term for Apple Macintosh.

★ **Nethead** – opposite of newbie: internet train spotter.

- ★ **Netiquette** – how to behave politely in online society.
- ★ **Netizen** – a person engaged in online social intercourse.
- ★ **Netlag** – when heavy traffic slows the web.
- ★ **Newbie** – internet virgin.
- ★ **Nomad brands** – elastic brands such as Virgin and Goldfish.
- ★ **Silver surfers** – surfers over 50.
- ★ **Site-seeing** – surfing.
- ★ **SoHo** – small office home office.
- ★ **Spam** – junk email.
- ★ **Sportal** – sports portal.
- ★ **Spurtal** – sex site.
- ★ **VC** – Vulture capitalist – otherwise known as venture capitalist.
- ★ **Vidiot** – early adopter of TV.
- ★ **Viral marketing** – low-cost marketing for internet businesses with no cash.
- ★ **Vortal** – vertical portal for a specific industry or interest group.
- ★ **We-commerce** – joint buying by web customers.
- ★ **Wetware** – hackers' term for human brain.
- ★ **Word of mouse** – internet gossip.
- ★ **WWW** – world wide wait.
- ★ **Yettie** – young entrepreneurial technically oriented twenty-something.

Internet homilies

- ★ 'To B2B or not to B2B'
- ★ 'Pebbles travel well on the web; boulders don't'
- ★ 'hardware giveth; software taketh away – substitute bandwidth and content'
- ★ 'TV is lean-back while PCs are lean-forward'